JAMESTOWN EDUCATION

AF271430

Timed Readings Plus
in Social Studies

BOOK 1

**25 Two-Part Lessons with Questions for
Building Reading Speed and Comprehension**

Glencoe

New York, New York   Columbus, Ohio   Chicago, Illinois   Peoria, Illinois   Woodland Hills, California

JAMESTOWN EDUCATION

 Glencoe

The **McGraw·Hill** Companies

ISBN: 0-07-845799-8

Send all queries to:
Glencoe/McGraw-Hill
8787 Orion Place
Columbus, OH 43240-4027

4 5 6 7 8 9 10 021 09

CONTENTS

TO THE STUDENT

You probably talk at an average rate of about 150 words a minute. If you are a reader of average ability, you read at a rate of about 250 words a minute. So your reading speed is nearly twice as fast as your speaking or listening speed. This example shows that reading is one of the fastest ways to get information.

The purpose of this book is to help you increase your reading rate and understand what you read. The 25 lessons in this book will also give you practice in reading social studies articles and in preparing for tests in which you must read and understand nonfiction passages within a certain time limit.

Reading Faster and Better

Following are some strategies that you can use to read the articles in each lesson.

Previewing

Previewing before you read is a very important step. This helps you to get an idea of what a selection is about and to recall any previous knowledge you have about the subject. Here are the steps to follow when previewing.

Read the title. Titles are designed not only to announce the subject but also to make the reader think. Ask yourself questions such as What can I learn from the title? What thoughts does it bring to mind?

What do I already know about this subject?

Read the first sentence. If they are short, read the first two sentences. The opening sentence is the writer's opportunity to get your attention. Some writers announce what they hope to tell you in the selection. Some writers state their purpose for writing; others just try to get your attention.

Read the last sentence. If it is short, read the final two sentences. The closing sentence is the writer's last chance to get ideas across to you. Some writers repeat the main idea once more. Some writers draw a conclusion—this is what they have been leading up to. Other writers summarize their thoughts; they tie all the facts together.

Skim the entire selection. Glance through the selection quickly to see what other information you can pick up. Look for anything that will help you read fluently and with understanding. Are there names, dates, or numbers? If so, you may have to read more slowly.

Reading for Meaning

Here are some ways to make sure you are making sense of what you read.

Build your concentration. You cannot understand what you read if you are not concentrating. When you discover that your thoughts are straying, correct the situation right away. Avoid distractions and distracting situations. Keep in mind the information you learned from previewing. This will help focus your attention on the selection.

Read in thought groups. Try to see meaningful combinations of words—phrases, clauses, or sentences. If you look at only one word at a time (called word-by-word reading), both your comprehension and your reading speed suffer.

Ask yourself questions. To sustain the pace you have set for yourself and to maintain a high level of concentration and comprehension, ask yourself questions such as What does this mean? or How can I use this information? as you read.

Finding the Main Ideas

The paragraph is the basic unit of meaning. If you can quickly discover and understand the main idea of each paragraph, you will build your comprehension of the selection.

Find the topic sentence. The topic sentence, which contains the main idea, often is the first sentence of a paragraph. It is followed by sentences that support, develop, or explain the main idea. Sometimes a topic sentence comes at the end of a paragraph. When it does, the supporting details come first, building the base for the topic sentence. Some paragraphs do not have a topic sentence; all of the sentences combine to create a meaningful idea.

Understand paragraph structure. Every well-written paragraph has a purpose. The purpose may be to inform, define, explain, or illustrate. The purpose should always relate to the main idea and expand on it. As you read each paragraph, see how the body of the paragraph tells you more about the main idea.

Relate ideas as you read. As you read the selection, notice how the writer puts together ideas. As you discover the relationship between the ideas, the main ideas come through quickly and clearly.

Mastering Reading Comprehension

Reading fast is not useful if you don't remember or understand what you read. The two exercises in Part A provide a check on how well you have understood the article.

Recalling Facts

These multiple-choice questions provide a quick check to see how well you recall important information from the article. As you learn to apply the reading strategies described earlier, you should be able to answer these questions more successfully.

Understanding Ideas

These questions require you to think about the main ideas in the article. Some main ideas are stated in the article; others are not. To answer some of the questions, you need to draw conclusions about what you read.

The five exercises in Part B require multiple answers. These exercises provide practice in applying comprehension and critical thinking skills that you can use in all your reading.

Recognizing Words in Context

Always check to see whether the words around an unfamiliar word—its context—can give you a clue to the word's meaning. A word generally appears in a context related to its meaning.

Suppose, for example, that you are unsure of the meaning of the word *expired* in the following passage:

> Vera wanted to check out a book, but her library card had expired. She had to borrow my card, because she didn't have time to renew hers.

You could begin to figure out the meaning of *expired* by asking yourself a question such as, What could have happened to Vera's library card that would make her need to borrow someone else's card? You might realize that if Vera had to renew her card, its usefulness must have come to an end or run out. This would lead you to conclude that the word *expired* must mean "to come to an end" or "to run out." You would be right. The context suggested the meaning.

Context can also affect the meaning of a word you already know. The word *key,* for instance, has many meanings. There are musical keys, door keys, and keys to solving a

mystery. The context in which the word *key* occurs will tell you which meaning is correct.

Sometimes a word is explained by the words that immediately follow it. The subject of a sentence and your knowledge about that subject might also help you determine the meaning of an unknown word. Try to decide the meaning of the word *revive* in the following sentence:

> Sunshine and water will revive those drooping plants.

The compound subject is *sunshine* and *water.* You know that plants need light and water to survive and that drooping plants are not healthy. You can figure out that *revive* means "to bring back to health."

Distinguishing Fact from Opinion

Every day you are called upon to sort out fact and opinion. Because much of what you read and hear contains both facts and opinions, you need to be able to tell the two apart.

Facts are statements that can be proved. The proof must be objective and verifiable. You must be able to check for yourself to confirm a fact.

Look at the following facts. Notice that they can be checked for accuracy and confirmed. Suggested sources for verification appear in parentheses.

- Abraham Lincoln was the 16th president of the United States. (Consult biographies, social studies books, encyclopedias, and similar sources.)

- Earth revolves around the Sun. (Research in encyclopedias or astronomy books; ask knowledgeable people.)

- Dogs walk on four legs. (See for yourself.)

Opinions are statements that cannot be proved. There is no objective evidence you can consult to check the truthfulness of an opinion. Unlike facts, opinions express personal beliefs or judgments. Opinions reveal how someone feels about a subject, not the facts about that subject. You might agree or disagree with someone's opinion, but you cannot prove it right or wrong.

Look at the following opinions. The reasons these statements are classified as opinions appear in parentheses.

- Abraham Lincoln was born to be a president. (You cannot prove this by referring to birth records. There is no evidence to support this belief.)

- Earth is the only planet in our solar system where intelligent life exists. (There is no proof of this. It may be proved true some day, but for now it is just an educated guess—not a fact.)

- The dog is a human's best friend. (This is not a fact; your best friend might not be a dog.)

As you read, be aware that facts and opinions are often mixed together. Both are useful to you as a reader. But to evaluate what you read and to read intelligently, you need to know the difference between the two.

Keeping Events in Order

Sequence, or chronological order, is the order of events in a story or article or the order of steps in a process. Paying attention to the sequence of events or steps will help you follow what is happening, predict what might happen next, and make sense of a passage.

To make the sequence as clear as possible, writers often use signal words to help the reader get a more exact idea of when things happen. Following is a list of frequently used signal words and phrases:

until	first
next	then
before	after
finally	later
when	while
during	now
at the end	by the time
as soon as	in the beginning

Signal words and phrases are also useful when a writer chooses to relate details or events out of sequence. You need to pay careful attention to determine the correct chronological order.

Making Correct Inferences

Much of what you read *suggests* more than it *says*. Writers often do not state ideas directly in a text. They can't. Think of the time and space it would take to state every idea. And think of how boring that would be! Instead, writers leave it to you, the reader, to fill in the information they leave out—to make inferences. You do this by combining clues in the story or article with knowledge from your own experience.

You make many inferences every day. Suppose, for example, that you are visiting a friend's house for the first time. You see a bag of kitty litter. You infer (make an inference) that the family has a cat. Another day you overhear a conversation. You catch the names of two actors and the words *scene, dialogue,* and *directing.* You infer that the people are discussing a movie or play.

In these situations and others like them, you infer unstated information from what you observe or read. Readers must make inferences in order to understand text.

Be careful about the inferences you make. One set of facts may suggest several inferences. Some of these inferences could be faulty. A correct inference must be supported by evidence.

Remember that bag of kitty litter that caused you to infer that your friend has a cat? That could be a faulty inference. Perhaps your friend's family uses the kitty litter on their icy sidewalks to create traction. To be sure your inference is correct, you need more evidence.

Understanding Main Ideas

The main idea is the most important idea in a paragraph or passage—the idea that provides purpose and direction. The rest of the selection explains, develops, or supports the main idea. Without a main idea, there would be only a collection of unconnected thoughts.

In the following paragraph, the main idea is printed in italics. As you read, observe how the other sentences develop or explain the main idea.

Typhoon Chris hit with full fury today on the central coast of Japan. Heavy rain from the storm flooded the area. High waves carried many homes into the sea. People now fear that the heavy rains will cause mudslides in the central part of the country. The number of people killed by the storm may climb past the 200 mark by Saturday.

In this paragraph, the main-idea statement appears first. It is followed by sentences that explain, support, or give details. Sometimes the main idea appears at the end of a paragraph. Writers often put the main idea at the end of a paragraph when their purpose is to persuade or convince. Readers may be more open to a new idea if the reasons for it are presented first.

As you read the following paragraph, think about the overall impact of the supporting ideas. Their purpose is to convince the reader that the main idea in the last sentence should be accepted.

Last week there was a head-on collision at Huntington and Canton streets. Just a month ago a pedestrian was struck there. Fortunately, she was only slightly injured. In the past year, there have been more accidents there than at any other corner in the city. In fact, nearly 10 percent of all accidents in the city occur at the corner. This intersection is very dangerous, and a traffic signal should be installed there before a life is lost.

The details in the paragraph progress from least important to most important. They achieve their full effect in the main idea statement at the end.

In many cases, the main idea is not expressed in a single sentence. The reader is called upon to interpret all of the ideas expressed in the paragraph and to decide upon a main idea. Read the following paragraph.

> The American author Jack London was once a pupil at the Cole Grammar School in Oakland, California. Each morning the class sang a song. When the teacher noticed that Jack wouldn't sing, she sent him to the principal. He returned to class with a note. The note said that Jack could be excused from singing with the class if he would write an essay every morning.

In this paragraph, the reader has to interpret the individual ideas and to decide on a main idea. This main idea seems reasonable: Jack London's career as a writer began with a punishment in grammar school.

Understanding the concept of the main idea and knowing how to find it is important. Transferring that understanding to your reading and study is also important.

Working Through a Lesson

Part A

1. **Preview the article.** Locate the timed selection in Part A of the lesson that you are going to read. Wait for your teacher's signal to preview. You will have 20 seconds for previewing. Follow the previewing steps described on page 2.

2. **Read the article.** When your teacher gives you the signal, begin reading. Read carefully so that you will be able to answer questions about what you have read. When you finish reading, look at the board and note your reading time. Write this time at the bottom of the page on the line labeled Reading Time.

3. **Complete the exercises.** Answer the 10 questions that follow the article. There are 5 fact questions and 5 idea questions. Choose the best answer to each question and put an X in that box.

4. **Correct your work.** Use the Answer Key at the back of the book to check your answers. Circle any wrong answer and put an X in the box you should have marked. Record the number of correct answers on the appropriate line at the end of the lesson.

Part B

1. **Preview and read the passage.** Use the same techniques you

used to read Part A. Think about what you are reading.

2. **Complete the exercises.** Instructions are given for answering each category of question. There are 15 responses for you to record.

3. **Correct your work.** Use the Answer Key at the back of the book. Circle any wrong answer and write the correct letter or number next to it. Record the number of correct answers on the appropriate line at the end of the lesson.

Plotting Your Progress

1. **Find your reading rate.** Turn to the Reading Rate graph on page 116. Put an X at the point where the vertical line that represents the lesson intersects your reading time, shown along the left-hand side. The right-hand side of the graph will reveal your words-per-minute reading speed.

2. **Find your comprehension score.** Add your scores for Part A and Part B to determine your total number of correct answers. Turn to the Comprehension Score Graph on page 117. Put an X at the point where the vertical line that represents your lesson intersects your total correct answers, shown along the left-hand side. The right-hand side of the graph will show the percentage of questions you answered correctly.

3. **Complete the Comprehension Skills Profile.** Turn to page 118. Record your incorrect answers for the Part B exercises. The five Part B skills are listed along the bottom. There are five columns of boxes, one column for each question. For every incorrect answer, put an X in a box for that skill.

To get the most benefit from these lessons, you need to take charge of your own progress in improving your reading speed and comprehension. Studying these graphs will help you to see whether your reading rate is increasing and to determine what skills you need to work on. Your teacher will also review the graphs to check your progress.

To the Teacher

About the Series

Timed Readings Plus in Social Studies includes 10 books at reading levels 4–13, with one book at each level. Book One contains material at a fourth-grade reading level; Book Two at a fifth-grade level, and so on. The readability level is determined by the Fry Readability Scale and is not to be confused with grade or age level of the student. The books are designed for use with students at middle school level and above.

The purposes of the series are as follows:

- to provide systematic, structured reading practice that helps students improve their reading rate and comprehension skills

- to give students practice in reading and understanding informational articles in the content area of social studies

- to give students experience in reading various text types—informational, expository, narrative, and prescriptive

- to prepare students for taking standardized tests that include timed reading passages in various content areas

- to provide materials with a wide range of reading levels so that students can continue to practice and improve their reading rate and comprehension skills

Because the books are designed for use with students at designated reading levels rather than in a particular grade, the social studies topics in this series are not correlated to any grade-level curriculum. Most standardized tests require students to read and comprehend social studies passages. This series provides an opportunity for students to become familiar with the particular requirements of reading social studies. For example, the vocabulary in a social studies article is important. Students need to know certain words in order to understand the concepts and the information.

Each book in the series contains 25 two-part lessons. Part A focuses on improving reading rate. This section of the lesson consists of a 400-word timed informational article on a social studies topic followed by two multiple-choice exercises. Recalling Facts includes five fact questions; Understanding Ideas includes five critical thinking questions.

Part B concentrates on building mastery in critical areas of comprehension. This section consists of a nontimed passage—the "plus" passage—followed by five exercises that address five major comprehension skills. The passage varies in length; its subject matter relates to the content of the timed selection.

Timed Reading and Comprehension

Timed reading is the best-known method of improving reading speed. There is no point in someone's reading at an accelerated speed if the person does not understand what she or he is reading. Nothing is more important than comprehension in reading. The main purpose of reading is to gain knowledge and insight, to understand the information that the writer and the text are communicating.

Few students will be able to read a passage once and answer all of the questions correctly. A score of 70 or 80 percent correct is normal. If the student gets 90 or 100 percent correct, he or she is either reading too slowly or the material is at too low a reading level. A comprehension or critical thinking score of less than 70 percent indicates a need for improvement.

One method of improving comprehension and critical thinking skills is for the student to go back and study each incorrect answer. First, the student should reread the question carefully. It is surprising how many students get the wrong answer simply because they have not read the question carefully. Then the student should look back in the passage to find the place where the question is answered, reread that part of the passage, and think about how to arrive at the correct answer. It is important to be able to recognize a correct answer when it is embedded in the text. Teacher guidance or class discussion will help the student find an answer.

Speed Versus Comprehension

It is not unusual for comprehension scores to decline as reading rate increases during the early weeks of timed readings. If this happens, students should attempt to level off their speed—but not lower it—and concentrate more on comprehension. Usually, if students maintain the higher speed and concentrate on comprehension, scores will gradually improve and within a week or two be back up to normal levels of 70 to 80 percent.

It is important to achieve a proper balance between speed and comprehension. An inefficient reader typically reads everything at one speed, usually slowly. Some poor readers, however, read rapidly but without satisfactory comprehension. It is important to achieve a balance between speed and comprehension. The practice that this series provides enables students to increase their reading speed while maintaining normal levels of comprehension.

Getting Started

As a rule, the passages in a book designed to improve reading speed should be relatively easy. The student should not have much difficulty with the vocabulary or the subject matter. Don't worry about the passages being too easy; students should see how quickly and efficiently they can read a passage.

Begin by assigning students to a level. A student should start with a book that is one level below his or her current reading level. If a student's reading level is not known, a suitable starting point would be one or two levels below the student's present grade in school.

Introduce students to the contents and format of the book they are using. Examine the book to see how it is organized. Talk about the parts of each lesson. Discuss the purpose of timed reading and the use of the progress graphs at the back of the book.

Timing the Reading

One suggestion for timing the reading is to have all students begin reading the selection at the same time. After one minute, write on the board the time that has elapsed and begin updating it at 10-second intervals (1:00, 1:10, 1:20, etc.). Another option is to have individual students time themselves with a stopwatch.

Teaching a Lesson

Part A

1. Give students the signal to begin previewing the lesson. Allow 20 seconds, then discuss special terms or vocabulary that students found.

2. Use one of the methods described above to time students as they read the passage. (Include the 20-second preview time as part of the first minute.) Tell students to write down the last time shown on the board or the stopwatch when they finish reading. Have them record the time in the designated space after the passage.

3. Next, have students complete the exercises in Part A. Work with them to check their answers, using the Answer Key that begins on page 114. Have them circle incorrect answers, mark the correct answers, and then record the numbers of correct answers for Part A on the appropriate line at the end of the lesson. Correct responses to eight or more questions indicate satisfactory comprehension and recall.

Part B

1. Have students read the Part B passage and complete the exercises that follow it. Directions are provided with each exercise. Correct responses require deliberation and discrimination.

2. Work with students to check their answers. Then discuss the answers with them and have them record the number of correct answers for Part B at the end of the lesson.

Have students study the correct answers to the questions they answered incorrectly. It is important that they understand why a particular answer is correct or incorrect.

Have them reread relevant parts of a passage to clarify an answer. An effective cooperative activity is to have students work in pairs to discuss their answers, explain why they chose the answers they did, and try to resolve differences.

Monitoring Progress

Have students find their total correct answers for the lesson and record their reading time and scores on the graphs on pages 116 and 117. Then have them complete the Comprehension Skills Profile on page 118. For each incorrect response to a question in Part B, students should mark an X in the box above each question type.

The legend on the Reading Rate graph automatically converts reading times to words-per-minute rates. The Comprehension Score graph automatically converts the raw scores to percentages.

These graphs provide a visual record of a student's progress. This record gives the student and you an opportunity to evaluate the student's progress and to determine the types of exercises and skills he or she needs to concentrate on.

Diagnosis and Evaluation

The following are typical reading rates.

Slow Reader—150 Words Per Minute

Average Reader—250 Words Per Minute

Fast Reader—350 Words Per Minute

A student who consistently reads at an average or above-average rate (with satisfactory comprehension) is ready to advance to the next book in the series.

A column of Xs in the Comprehension Skills Profile indicates a specific comprehension weakness. Using the profile, you can assess trends in student performance and suggest remedial work if necessary.

1 A George Washington: The Father of Our Country

George Washington was the first president of the United States. He is known as the Father of Our Country. He is called this because so much of his life was spent in service to America.

Washington was born in Virginia in 1732. He grew to be a tall, strong boy. As a teen, his older brother, Lawrence, helped him learn to survey land. When he was 17, he became county surveyor. When Lawrence died, George took over his job in the militia. George was given the rank of major. He had to gather and inspect the troops. Washington was a strong leader, so he was put in charge of all of Virginia's troops. For three years, he defended Virginia's west border. He also was a leader in the French and Indian War.

In 1759 he returned home to his farm, Mount Vernon. He set up a mill and an ironworks. He married a widow, Martha Custis. He also served in state government. He opposed many British policies. One of these policies was the Stamp Act. This was a British law that taxed the colonies without their consent. Washington thought that Britain's rule was not good for the colonies. He felt that America should govern itself.

When the Revolutionary War broke out in 1775, Washington was made commander in chief of the Continental Army. His troops had had no training. He had few supplies. His plan was to have patience and to harass the British at every chance. In battle, he would fall back at first. Then he would launch a surprise strike. After six years, he forced the British to give up.

People felt that Washington was a hero. They wanted him to be the first president. Some even wanted to make him king. He did not want to be president. He wanted to go home. He wanted to spend the rest of his life working on his farm. However, Washington knew that the first president would pave the way for the future. He wanted to help form the nation he had served so well. So in 1789, he took the oath of office.

Washington served as president for eight years. During that time, France was at war with Britain. Washington kept the United States out of war. He knew the country needed time to grow strong. After eight years in office, he went back to Mount Vernon and farmed until he died.

Reading Time _____

Recalling Facts

1. George Washington was
   - ❏ a. the king.
   - ❏ b. a Navy officer.
   - ❏ c. commander in chief of the Continental Army.

2. The colonies won their freedom in a war with
   - ❏ a. France.
   - ❏ b. Britain.
   - ❏ c. Native Americans.

3. Washington was born in
   - ❏ a. Britain.
   - ❏ b. Virginia.
   - ❏ c. New York.

4. Washington's plan to win the war was to
   - ❏ a. attack the British at sea.
   - ❏ b. launch an all-out attack.
   - ❏ c. have patience and harass the British.

5. Washington served as president for
   - ❏ a. four years.
   - ❏ b. eight years.
   - ❏ c. twelve years.

Understanding Ideas

6. Washington is called the Father of Our Country because
   - ❏ a. he opposed the Stamp Act.
   - ❏ b. he commanded the colonial army.
   - ❏ c. he led the colonies' fight for freedom and he was the first U.S. president.

7. From the passage, one can infer that George Washington
   - ❏ a. wanted power.
   - ❏ b. was not popular.
   - ❏ c. put serving his country above his own needs.

8. From the passage, one can infer that Washington
   - ❏ a. had many skills.
   - ❏ b. disliked farming.
   - ❏ c. was a brilliant military leader but knew little about government.

9. Washington probably took the job of president because
   - ❏ a. no one else would do the job.
   - ❏ b. he had wanted it for a long time.
   - ❏ c. his country needed his leadership.

10. The statement "the first president would pave the way for the future" probably means that he would
   - ❏ a. write all of the country's laws.
   - ❏ b. set an example for future presidents.
   - ❏ c. build new roads that could be used then and in the future.

Mount Vernon

Mount Vernon is the magnificent home of George Washington. It stands on a hill in Virginia. The house, which is made of wood, is three stories tall. It was built by George's older brother, Lawrence. It was passed on to George by Lawrence's widow. At that time, the house had two floors and seven rooms. It was on 2,000 acres of land. Washington built a third floor and added new furnishings. After he married Martha Custis, she and her two children moved to Mount Vernon. She and George added north and south wings to the house.

The whole time Washington lived at Mount Vernon, he worked to make it a grand home. The two-story porch on the front of the mansion is his design. He built a cupola (small domed structure) above the roof. From there, one can see the Potomac River. On top of the cupola, he placed a weathervane. It is called the Dove of Peace. He rebuilt the gardens and lanes. He increased the size of the estate to 8,000 acres. More than 300 enslaved persons worked the plantation. Washington freed many of them when he died. Now the estate is owned by the Mount Vernon Ladies' Association. They keep the home much as it was in Washington's time.

1. Recognizing Words in Context

Find the word *magnificent* in the passage. One definition below is closest to the meaning of that word. One definition has the opposite or nearly the opposite meaning. The remaining definition has a completely different meaning. Label the definitions C for *closest,* O for *opposite or nearly opposite,* and D for *different.*

_____ a. tired

_____ b. great

_____ c. ordinary

2. Distinguishing Fact from Opinion

Two of the statements below present *facts,* which can be proved. The other statement is an *opinion,* which expresses someone's thoughts or beliefs. Label the statements F for *fact* and O for *opinion.*

_____ a. From the cupola, one can see the Potomac River.

_____ b. Mount Vernon is the home of George Washington.

_____ c. Mount Vernon should belong to the U.S. government.

3. Keeping Events in Order

Number the statements below 1, 2, and 3 to show the order in which the events took place.

_____ a. George Washington built a third floor.

_____ b. Lawrence Washington built Mount Vernon.

_____ c. The Washingtons added north and south wings to the house.

4. Making Correct Inferences

Two of the statements below are correct *inferences*, or reasonable guesses. They are based on information in the passage. The other statement is an incorrect, or faulty, inference. Label the statements C for *correct* inference and F for *faulty* inference.

_____ a. Washington was not interested in making improvements to his Mount Vernon home.

_____ b. Washington greatly increased the size of Mount Vernon.

_____ c. People who visit Mount Vernon can learn about history.

5. Understanding Main Ideas

One of the statements below expresses the main idea of the passage. One statement is too general, or too broad. The other explains only part of the passage; it is too narrow. Label the statements M for *main idea*, B for *too broad*, and N for *too narrow*.

_____ a. Mount Vernon is one of many historic buildings in Virginia.

_____ b. The weathervane on top of the cupola is called the Dove of Peace.

_____ c. Mount Vernon was a large plantation and the home of George and Martha Washington.

Correct Answers, Part A _____

Correct Answers, Part B _____

Total Correct Answers _____

The Birch Bark Canoe: A Native American Invention

Long ago traveling through the thick forests of North America was a problem. There were no roads. However, there were chains of lakes, rivers, and streams. On the banks of these waterways grew pine, spruce, cedar, and birch trees. Birch trees have white or gray bark that peels off in sheets. The ancient Native American peoples learned how to use these trees to build boats. They did not build just any boats—they built birch bark canoes.

Rapids are places where water moves at great speed because a river drops. Rapids are a problem for boats. While going over rapids, a boat can be smashed if it hits the rocks. But a canoe is small and light. A person can carry, or portage, a canoe around rapids or from one stream to another.

A canoe is a narrow boat with curved sides. The sides are widest in the middle. They come together at the bow (front) and at the stern (back). The ends of the canoe have a rounded shape. Canoes are propelled and steered through the water with paddles.

When making a birch bark canoe, Native Americans peeled sheets of bark from birch trees. They then laid the sheets out on a flat piece of ground. The gunwales (upper edges) of the canoe were made of wood that was bent to the shape of the canoe. The gunwale frame was laid on top of the bark. The edges of the bark were wrapped around the gunwales. Next the birch bark was weighed down with rocks. Then the builders drove wooden stakes into the ground around the gunwales. The stakes helped to shape the canoe as it was being built. Then the gunwales were raised to the correct height and held in place.

The seams of the bark were sewn together with spruce root. The builders used pine gum, spruce resin (sap), and animal fat to make the seams watertight. They lined the inside of the canoe with thin sheets of cedar. The lining was held in place by ribs of cedar. The builders cut these ribs and bent them to the shape of the canoe.

When the canoe was finished, an animal was sometimes carved on the outside. Often this was a symbol of the tribe. It took two people—usually a man and a woman—two weeks to build a birch bark canoe.

Reading Time _____

Recalling Facts

1. Rapids are found where
   - ❏ a. two rivers meet.
   - ❏ b. a river flows into a lake.
   - ❏ c. a river drops and water rushes at great speed.

2. Trees that have white or gray bark that peels off in sheets are called
   - ❏ a. pine trees.
   - ❏ b. birch trees.
   - ❏ c. spruce trees.

3. Carrying a canoe overland from one stream to the next is a
   - ❏ a. stern.
   - ❏ b. portage.
   - ❏ c. gunwale.

4. The seams of a birch bark canoe were sewn together with
   - ❏ a. pine gum.
   - ❏ b. cedar ribs.
   - ❏ c. spruce root.

5. Two persons could build a birch bark canoe in
   - ❏ a. two weeks.
   - ❏ b. three weeks.
   - ❏ c. seven weeks.

Understanding Ideas

6. Compared with walking through the forests, canoe travel was
   - ❏ a. faster.
   - ❏ b. slower.
   - ❏ c. more dangerous.

7. From the passage, one can infer that birch bark canoes are
   - ❏ a. wide at the ends.
   - ❏ b. shaped the same at both ends.
   - ❏ c. wider in the back than in the front.

8. Birch bark was most likely used on a canoe to make it
   - ❏ a. fast.
   - ❏ b. white or gray in color.
   - ❏ c. strong and lightweight.

9. It is most likely that Native Americans carved animals on their canoes to
   - ❏ a. bring good luck.
   - ❏ b. show ownership.
   - ❏ c. keep their enemies away.

10. Which of the following sentences best tells what the whole passage is about?
    - ❏ a. Traveling through the forests was a problem.
    - ❏ b. Sheets of bark were peeled from birch trees.
    - ❏ c. Ancient Native Americans invented the birch bark canoe.

To build a model of a birch bark canoe, first gather the materials. Peel off a length of birch bark from a birch log or dead birch tree. Do not peel bark from a live birch tree. If birch bark is not available from a dead tree, use paper. A piece of typing paper or a brown bag will work. A pair of scissors and white glue are needed too.

Step one: Use the scissors to cut a three-inch by five-inch strip of bark or paper.

Step two: Cut the lengthwise ends of the bark or paper to make a *V*. The *V* should be about one-half inch deep.

Step three: Fold the bark or paper in half, lengthwise.

Step four: Overlap the two edges made from cutting the *V* at each end. Place them so that the top edges are even with each other. This is the top edge of the canoe.

Step five: Glue the edges together with white glue. Hold them securely in place so they don't move until the glue dries.

Step six: If using birch bark, try the model canoe out in a sink or a bowl of water. The model will float. A paper model may float for a little while.

Remember, always make sure to ask an adult to help when using scissors.

1. **Recognizing Words in Context**

   Find the word *securely* in the passage. One definition below is closest to the meaning of that word. One definition has the opposite or nearly the opposite meaning. The remaining definition has a completely different meaning. Label the definitions C for *closest*, O for *opposite or nearly opposite*, and D for *different*.

   _____ a. unevenly

   _____ b. loosely

   _____ c. tightly

2. **Distinguishing Fact from Opinion**

   Two of the statements below present *facts*, which can be proved. The other statement is an *opinion*, which expresses someone's thoughts or beliefs. Label the statements F for *fact* and O for *opinion*.

   _____ a. A model canoe made of birch bark will float.

   _____ b. Model canoes should be made of birch bark, not paper.

   _____ c. A model birch bark canoe can be made using birch bark or paper, scissors, and glue.

3. **Keeping Events in Order**

   Number the statements below 1, 2, and 3 to show the order in which the events took place.

   _____ a. Gather the materials.

   _____ b. Cut the lengthwise ends of the bark or paper to make a *V*.

   _____ c. Overlap the two edges made from cutting the *V* at each end.

4. **Making Correct Inferences**

   Two of the statements below are correct *inferences,* or reasonable guesses. They are based on information in the passage. The other statement is an incorrect, or faulty, inference. Label the statements C for *correct* inference and F for *faulty* inference.

   _____ a. A model of a birch bark canoe can be made easily with few materials.

   _____ b. It takes several days to make a model of a birch bark canoe.

   _____ c. Peeling bark from a live birch tree could hurt the tree.

5. **Understanding Main Ideas**

   One of the statements below expresses the main idea of the passage. One statement is too general, or too broad. The other explains only part of the passage; it is too narrow. Label the statements M for *main idea,* B for *too broad,* and N for *too narrow.*

   _____ a. Model boats can be made from many kinds of materials.

   _____ b. If birch bark is not available from a dead tree, use paper.

   _____ c. Follow these steps to make a model birch bark canoe from birch bark or paper.

Correct Answers, Part A _____

Correct Answers, Part B _____

Total Correct Answers _____

Making Coins at the U.S. Mint

The main purpose of the U.S. Mint is to make coins for use in business and trade. But the mint also makes special coins. Some of these are uncirculated coin sets, proof sets, and commemorative coins. Uncirculated coins are coins that have not been used. Proof sets are sets of coins that have been polished and sealed in plastic. Commemorative coins honor American history and culture. Part of the money people use to buy commemorative coins goes to good causes. All these special coins can be spent. But they are made to be collected.

Coins are made at four mints. These are in Philadelphia, Pennsylvania; Denver, Colorado; San Francisco, California; and West Point, New York. Each of these mints makes special coins. The Philadelphia and Denver mints also make coins for circulation.

The mints make six kinds of regular coins. They are the penny, nickel, dime, quarter, half-dollar, and dollar coins. Most coins have portraits on one side. The portraits are usually of U.S. presidents. Some of the dollar coins have portraits of famous American women. State quarters—one for each of the 50 states—are now being made. Each state quarter honors one state.

The mints make coins from blanks, which are called planchets. A blank is a metal circle, the right size and thickness for the coin. The mints buy blanks to make pennies, but they make their own nickel blanks. Penny and nickel blanks are made by melting metals together to make an alloy. (An alloy is a mixture of two or more metals.) The liquid alloy is then poured into molds. The molds shape the metal into blocks, called ingots. Coin makers roll the ingots into strips. Then they cut blanks from the strips. Dimes, quarters, half-dollars, and dollars have copper cores. An alloy covers this core. By looking at the edge of the coin, the core can be seen. The mint makes blanks for these coins from metal strips.

To make coins from blanks, workers first soften and clean the blanks. They then roll the edges to make them thicker. Finally the designs are stamped on each side. Dimes, quarters, half-dollars, and dollars get ridged edges. Workers then check the coins, count them, and put them into bags. Each bag is checked by weighing it. The mints ship the coins to the Federal Reserve Banks. From there, the coins are sent to other banks so they can go into circulation.

Reading Time _____

Recalling Facts

1. The main purpose of the U.S. Mint is to
   - ❑ a. raise money for good causes.
   - ❑ b. make coins for use in business and trade.
   - ❑ c. make special coins to honor famous people.

2. Coins are made at _____ mints.
   - ❑ a. two
   - ❑ b. four
   - ❑ c. three

3. Coins for circulation are made at the
   - ❑ a. West Point mint.
   - ❑ b. Philadelphia and Denver mints.
   - ❑ c. San Francisco and West Point mints.

4. Blanks used to make coins are also called
   - ❑ a. ingots.
   - ❑ b. alloys.
   - ❑ c. planchets.

5. After the mints make new coins, they ship them to
   - ❑ a. local banks.
   - ❑ b. the Federal Reserve Banks.
   - ❑ c. stores in many parts of the country.

Understanding Ideas

6. A coin that celebrates the Olympics is most likely a
   - ❑ a. proof coin.
   - ❑ b. regular coin.
   - ❑ c. commemorative coin.

7. Of the following, the easiest way for people to tell a dime from a penny with their eyes closed is to
   - ❑ a. feel the edges of the coins.
   - ❑ b. pick each coin up from a flat surface.
   - ❑ c. use a magnet to see which coin is picked up.

8. A quarter is most likely made at which mint?
   - ❑ a. Denver
   - ❑ b. West Point
   - ❑ c. San Francisco

9. Which of the following can *not* be spent at a store?
   - ❑ a. a state quarter
   - ❑ b. a nickel blank
   - ❑ c. a proof half-dollar

10. The most likely reason the mints weigh each bag of coins is to make sure that
   - ❑ a. the correct kind of coin is in the bag.
   - ❑ b. each bag has the correct number of coins.
   - ❑ c. the bag contains actual coins, not blanks.

Susan B. Anthony was born in 1820. She grew up in New York, where she began teaching school at 15. At 29, she became a reformer. She was against drinking liquor, and she worked to help end slavery. She also became a suffragist. This means she felt that women should have the same voting rights as men. After the war, she helped found the National Woman Suffrage Association. Its goal was to amend the U.S. Constitution so that women could vote. She worked for the rest of her life to gain the vote.

In 1979 the United States honored Anthony by putting her face on a dollar coin. This was the first time that a woman's portrait was shown on U.S. money. Anthony's face is on the front of the coin. The coin is made from copper and nickel over a copper core. The U.S. Mint felt that the coin would replace the dollar bill. It did not turn out that way. The coin is very close in size to a quarter. Many people thought it was easy to confuse the two coins. The mint stopped making the Susan B. Anthony dollar in 1981. But some vending machines were built to take the coin, so some people wanted the coins for the machines. The mint made more "Susies" in 1999.

1. **Recognizing Words in Context**

   Find the word *amend* in the passage. One definition below is closest to the meaning of that word. One definition has the opposite or nearly the opposite meaning. The remaining definition has a completely different meaning. Label the definitions C for *closest*, O for *opposite or nearly opposite*, and D for *different*.

   _____ a. remove

   _____ b. change

   _____ c. keep

2. **Distinguishing Fact from Opinion**

   Two of the statements below present *facts*, which can be proved. The other statement is an *opinion*, which expresses someone's thoughts or beliefs. Label the statements F for *fact* and O for *opinion*.

   _____ a. Anthony's face is on the front of a dollar coin.

   _____ b. Dollar bills should be replaced by dollar coins.

   _____ c. Anthony was a reformer and a suffragist.

3. Keeping Events in Order

Number the statements below 1, 2, and 3 to show the order in which the events took place.

_____ a. Anthony fought against slavery.

_____ b. Anthony taught school in New York.

_____ c. Anthony helped found the National Woman Suffrage Association.

4. Making Correct Inferences

Two of the statements below are correct *inferences*, or reasonable guesses. They are based on information in the passage. The other statement is an incorrect, or faulty, inference. Label the statements C for *correct* inference and F for *faulty* inference.

_____ a. The Susan B. Anthony dollar was not popular.

_____ b. Susan B. Anthony dollars were first made for vending machines.

_____ c. Throughout most of her life, Susan B. Anthony worked for good causes.

5. Understanding Main Ideas

One of the statements below expresses the main idea of the passage. One statement is too general, or too broad. The other explains only part of the passage; it is too narrow. Label the statements M for *main idea*, B for *too broad*, and N for *too narrow*.

_____ a. The Susan B. Anthony dollar is a coin that honors a famous suffragist.

_____ b. The Susan B. Anthony dollar has a core of pure copper.

_____ c. Commemorative coins honor important people.

Correct Answers, Part A _____

Correct Answers, Part B _____

Total Correct Answers _____

The Key Responsibilities of Local Government

There are five main levels of local government. One of these is county. States are divided into counties. A county is usually run by a board of local people. Two other levels of local government are township (or town) and city. The fourth level of local government is school district. School districts do not always have the same borders as townships or cities. A large city may have more than one school district. A school district may take in more than one township. The fifth level of local government is special district. This is set up to meet a specific need.

Local governments provide many services. They collect taxes to get money to pay for these services. One service is transportation. Counties and towns build and take care of the local roads. A city must maintain its streets. This includes snow and storm cleanup. Some cities have subways or bus lines that need to be cared for.

Law enforcement is a part of local government. A county might have a sheriff and deputies. A city often has a police force. These law officers enforce the laws and fight crime. There are district, county, and city courts. These courts hear cases. They decide if a person is guilty of breaking a law. They decide how the person should be punished. Communities also have fire departments. Fire departments need fire stations and equipment, such as fire trucks. Large cities may have paid firefighters who work full-time. A township might have volunteer firefighters. They are not paid, and they usually work at other jobs.

Local governments provide safe places to play. They pay for and care for parks with playgrounds, sport fields, or pools. Local governments also provide special services for their citizens. They pick up the garbage and provide clean water. They might tell where and how homes may be built. They may have a master plan. This plan shows where businesses and homes may be located. Laws, called building codes, state how homes must be built to make sure they are safe.

School districts run the local schools. They hire the teachers and build new schools as needed. A school board receives tax money to pay for the schools. Board members decide how that money should be spent. A special district may run the public libraries. These libraries are free for those who live in the district.

Reading Time _____

Recalling Facts

1. There are _____ main levels of local government.
   - ❏ a. five
   - ❏ b. three
   - ❏ c. eight

2. States are divided into
   - ❏ a. cities.
   - ❏ b. towns.
   - ❏ c. counties.

3. Special districts are set up to
   - ❏ a. meet a specific need.
   - ❏ b. repair city streets and buses.
   - ❏ c. run fire and police departments.

4. A city takes care of
   - ❏ a. city streets.
   - ❏ b. county roads.
   - ❏ c. national highways.

5. Volunteer firefighters
   - ❏ a. are paid by the school district.
   - ❏ b. work mostly in large cities.
   - ❏ c. are not paid.

Understanding Ideas

6. Which of the following sentences best tells what the whole passage is about?
   - ❏ a. A county is one level of local government.
   - ❏ b. Law enforcement is a part of local government.
   - ❏ c. Local governments provide many services to communities.

7. From the passage, one can infer that local taxes are used to
   - ❏ a. pay for state roads.
   - ❏ b. benefit the people who pay them.
   - ❏ c. care for all people who live in the state.

8. A house could not be located in both a
   - ❏ a. town and a city.
   - ❏ b. city and a county.
   - ❏ c. school district and a special district.

9. The local government most likely to provide the most services
   - ❏ a. has volunteer firefighters.
   - ❏ b. collects the most tax money.
   - ❏ c. provides public transportation.

10. A traffic ticket for speeding on a city street will most likely come from a
    - ❏ a. sheriff.
    - ❏ b. deputy.
    - ❏ c. police officer.

Firefighters are trained professionals who save lives and property. They go into burning buildings. They rescue people who are trapped, scared, or hurt. They teach fire safety in the schools. They save people trapped in car wrecks and cave-ins. Some are also Emergency Medical Technicians (EMTs). They are trained to help people who are hurt or ill. They help to keep people alive in route to a hospital.

What kind of person becomes a firefighter? The person must be strong and healthy enough to lift heavy loads, climb ladders, and crawl through smoke. He or she must have a sharp mind and calm nerves. This hard job must be done in the face of fires, earthquakes, floods, and accidents.

Who can be a firefighter? Each city or town sets its own standards. But everyone who wants to be a firefighter must finish high school. Then comes special training. EMT classes teach first-aid skills. College classes might include science, math, and building construction. These classes are needed to earn a fire science certificate. Then there are written and oral tests. If they are passed, there is an agility test. This test shows strength and endurance. Once a person is hired, training goes on. Firefighters must learn street names and numbers and the location of schools, factories, and tall buildings.

1. **Recognizing Words in Context**

Find the word *rescue* in the passage. One definition below is closest to the meaning of that word. One definition has the opposite or nearly the opposite meaning. The remaining definition has a completely different meaning. Label the definitions C for *closest*, O for *opposite or nearly opposite,* and D for *different*.

_____ a. lose

_____ b. save

_____ c. teach

2. **Distinguishing Fact from Opinion**

Two of the statements below present *facts,* which can be proved. The other statement is an *opinion,* which expresses someone's thoughts or beliefs. Label the statements F for *fact* and O for *opinion*.

_____ a. Some firefighters are also EMTs.

_____ b. More women should be firefighters.

_____ c. Each city or town sets its own standards for firefighters.

3. Keeping Events in Order

Number the statements below 1, 2, and 3 to show the order in which the events took place.

_____ a. A person applies for a job as a firefighter.

_____ b. A person goes to firefighting training.

_____ c. A person finishes high school.

4. Making Correct Inferences

Two of the statements below are correct *inferences,* or reasonable guesses. They are based on information in the passage. The other statement is an incorrect, or faulty, inference. Label the statements C for *correct* inference and F for *faulty* inference.

_____ a. Firefighters spend most of their time in classrooms.

_____ b. Firefighting is a dangerous job.

_____ c. Firefighters are heroes.

5. Understanding Main Ideas

One of the statements below expresses the main idea of the passage. One statement is too general, or too broad. The other explains only part of the passage; it is too narrow. Label the statements M for *main idea,* B for *too broad,* and N for *too narrow.*

_____ a. Firefighters teach fire safety in the schools.

_____ b. Firefighters are community helpers.

_____ c. Firefighters are trained professionals who save lives and property.

Correct Answers, Part A _____

Correct Answers, Part B _____

Total Correct Answers _____

The Nature of Farming in the United States Today

In the United States today, farms are getting larger in size but fewer in number. In colonial America, most people lived on farms. Now less than two percent of the people live on farms.

There are many reasons that fewer people live on farms. One reason is the growth of factories. People moved from farms to cities because jobs were available. Another reason is the use of machines on the farm. One of the first farm machines was the McCormick reaper. It reduced the labor needed to harvest wheat. More farm machines followed. They could do bigger jobs with fewer workers. Another change is that more food can be grown per acre. This is because of new strains of crops and better farming methods.

Farming has moved into world trade. Farmers grow more food than is needed in the United States. They sell some of what they produce overseas. But they must sell at prices that can compete in the world market. Large farms can produce more at a lower cost. They can get better buys on inputs, such as seed and fertilizer. Large farms use the latest farm machines to work more acres. Where do large farms get more land? They buy up farms that go out of business, or they rent land. A farm of 4,000 acres might actually be several small farms spread over several counties.

Small and medium-size farms cannot compete with large farms in the world market. In the past 20 years, many medium-size farms have disappeared. The farms have either grown in size or been sold. But the number of small farms has stayed about the same. How do small farms survive? The farmers have other means of income. They may work other jobs so they can run their farms on the side. They choose to farm even though profits are not high. Small farms have found their own markets. They may specialize in organic milk or fancy jams. Some sell directly to the public. They might have a roadside stand, a petting farm, a gift shop, or a cider mill. Sometimes small farms band together to work like a large farm. They may form a cooperative to buy farm machines. They may buy inputs in large amounts. Some small farms may form a larger corporation. Small, medium, or large, about 99 percent of U.S. farms are still owned by families.

Reading Time _____

Recalling Facts

1. Today less than _____ percent of the people in the United States live on farms.
   - ❏ a. two
   - ❏ b. five
   - ❏ c. fifteen

2. Today more food is grown per acre because of the
   - ❏ a. growth of factories.
   - ❏ b. increase in workers.
   - ❏ c. new strains of crops and better farming methods.

3. Inputs are things such as
   - ❏ a. seed and fertilizer.
   - ❏ b. new strains of crops.
   - ❏ c. large farm machines.

4. Large farms get more land by
   - ❏ a. buying land overseas.
   - ❏ b. taking land from cities.
   - ❏ c. buying farms that go out of business or by renting land.

5. One reason that small farms have survived is that they
   - ❏ a. rent more land.
   - ❏ b. have found their own markets.
   - ❏ c. compete well in the world market.

Understanding Ideas

6. Which of the following sentences best tells what the whole passage is about?
   - ❏ a. Farmers produce food.
   - ❏ b. In the United States today, there are fewer farmers who produce more food.
   - ❏ c. Small farms may form a larger cooperative and pool money to buy farm machines and inputs.

7. From the passage, one can infer that the McCormick reaper
   - ❏ a. was used on colonial farms.
   - ❏ b. required many workers to operate.
   - ❏ c. began a revolution in farm machines.

8. Probably small farmers who have other jobs continue to farm because
   - ❏ a. they love farming.
   - ❏ b. they are unable to sell their land.
   - ❏ c. they hope to grow into large farms.

9. A farm that sells at a farmers' market in the city is most likely a
   - ❏ a. large farm.
   - ❏ b. small farm.
   - ❏ c. medium farm.

10. To run a small farm, a farmer needs
    - ❏ a. 4,000 acres.
    - ❏ b. many workers.
    - ❏ c. some farm machinery.

The McCormick Reaper

In the early 1800s, it took a lot of manual labor to harvest wheat. First, the wheat was cut with a cradle. This was a long wooden handle with a cutting blade and wooden fingers. The farmer swung the cradle side to side. The blade cut the wheat, and the fingers held it. The farmer dropped the stalks of wheat in piles. Next, the stalks were tied in bundles. Finally, the bundles were stood up in groups, called shocks. One worker could cradle about two acres per day. After the grain dried, it was threshed, or removed from the stalks.

About 1831 Cyrus McCormick of Virginia invented a mechanical reaper. It was pulled by a horse. Blades moved back and forth to cut the grain. A wide wheel supported the machine as it rolled along. The wheel turned a reel that pushed the cut grain onto a platform. One worker rode the horse. Another raked the grain from the platform. The reaper could cut as much grain in one day as five workers could cut with cradles. McCormick moved to Chicago and started a company. He improved his machine. His Harvester and Binder cut grain and bound it with twine. Today's farm machines can cut 50 acres per day. They can also thresh the grain and clean it.

1. Recognizing Words in Context

Find the word *manual* in the passage. One definition below is closest to the meaning of that word. One definition has the opposite or nearly the opposite meaning. The remaining definition has a completely different meaning. Label the definitions C for *closest*, O for *opposite or nearly opposite*, and D for *different*.

_____ a. done quickly

_____ b. done by hand

_____ c. done by machine

2. Distinguishing Fact from Opinion

Two of the statements below present *facts*, which can be proved. The other statement is an *opinion*, which expresses someone's thoughts or beliefs. Label the statements F for *fact* and O for *opinion*.

_____ a. McCormick was the best inventor in the United States.

_____ b. In the early 1800s, wheat was cut with a cradle.

_____ c. About 1831 Cyrus McCormick invented a mechanical reaper.

3. **Keeping Events in Order**

Number the statements below 1, 2, and 3 to show the order in which the events took place.

_____ a. Workers stood the bundles in groups called shocks.

_____ b. Workers tied the grain in bundles by hand.

_____ c. Workers cut the wheat with a cradle.

4. **Making Correct Inferences**

Two of the statements below are correct *inferences,* or reasonable guesses. They are based on information in the passage. The other statement is an incorrect, or faulty, inference. Label the statements C for *correct* inference and F for *faulty* inference.

_____ a. Harvesting grain has many steps.

_____ b. It was easy to cut wheat with a hand cradle.

_____ c. The McCormick reaper led to today's farm machines.

5. **Understanding Main Ideas**

One of the statements below expresses the main idea of the passage. One statement is too general, or too broad. The other explains only part of the passage; it is too narrow. Label the statements M for *main idea*, B for *too broad*, and N for *too narrow.*

_____ a. Cyrus McCormick invented a mechanical reaper that made harvesting grain easier and faster.

_____ b. Cyrus McCormick of Virginia moved to Chicago and started a company.

_____ c. The McCormick reaper was the first of many farm machines.

Correct Answers, Part A _____

Correct Answers, Part B _____

Total Correct Answers _____

6 A   The One-Room Schoolhouse of the Nineteenth Century

In the United States in the nineteenth century, many children were taught in one-room schoolhouses. Grades one through eight shared the same classroom. A typical one-room schoolhouse was built of wood and painted white or red.

To get to school, children walked, rode a horse, or rode in a buggy. When it was time for school to begin, the teacher rang a bell. The children then went inside. Sometimes they stopped in a small room to wash their hands. They poured water from a pitcher into a bowl, called a basin. They hung their coats on hooks in a cloakroom and then went to their desks. They stood to recite the Pledge of Allegiance. The smallest children sat in the smallest desks at the front of the room, nearest the teacher's desk. The tallest children sat in the back. In the middle of the room stood a potbellied stove. It was used for heat on cold days. Those near the stove may have felt too warm. Those farthest away may have felt cold. The stove burned fuel, such as wood or coal.

The subjects taught were arithmetic, geography, science, history, reading, art, and penmanship. Students learned to write beautiful flowing script that was easy to read. Teachers wrote lessons on a blackboard at the front of the room. That is also where students worked math problems or practiced writing. In some schools, students had their own small slates to write on. Because one teacher had to teach all grade levels, the children were often taught one at a time.

Children were expected to be well behaved. Those who were not were punished by the teacher. The teacher may have used a leather strap, wooden cane, or wooden paddle for this purpose. Sometimes a child who had misbehaved would have to cut a switch from a tree, which the teacher would use on him or her. At noon, there was a recess. The children played and ate lunch. Students often carried their lunch to school in metal pails. In very cold weather, the teacher might cook something hot on the stove. Lessons resumed in the afternoon. When school let out, the children went home. There was rarely homework. Children were expected to help at home or do farm chores. Only a few children owned books. Books carried to and from school were wrapped by a leather strap and carried by the loose end of the strap.

Reading Time _____

Recalling Facts

1. In a one-room schoolhouse, children in grades one through eight
   - ❏ a. had different teachers.
   - ❏ b. shared the same classroom.
   - ❏ c. were taught the same lessons.

2. In the middle of the classroom stood
   - ❏ a. a potbellied stove.
   - ❏ b. the teacher's desk.
   - ❏ c. a pitcher and basin.

3. Students often carried their lunches to school in
   - ❏ a. metal pails.
   - ❏ b. paper sacks.
   - ❏ c. wooden buckets.

4. There was _____ homework.
   - ❏ a. never
   - ❏ b. rarely
   - ❏ c. always

5. A student who had books carried them
   - ❏ a. in a metal pail.
   - ❏ b. inside of a basin.
   - ❏ c. by a leather strap.

Understanding Ideas

6. Which of the following sentences best tells what the whole passage is about?
   - ❏ a. The blackboard was an important teaching tool.
   - ❏ b. In the nineteenth century, many children were taught in one-room schoolhouses.
   - ❏ c. In the United States, classrooms have changed a great deal over time.

7. The smallest children sat in the front of the classroom so that
   - ❏ a. all students could see the blackboard.
   - ❏ b. the oldest children could be the first to leave.
   - ❏ c. the smallest children would be the closest to the stove.

8. From the passage, one can infer that a potbellied stove
   - ❏ a. kept everyone comfortable.
   - ❏ b. did not heat the room very evenly.
   - ❏ c. was used mostly for cooking during the school day.

9. From the passage, one can infer that most children read
   - ❏ a. many books.
   - ❏ b. often at home.
   - ❏ c. usually only at school.

10. Students in a one-room school studied often
    - ❏ a. in a group.
    - ❏ b. on their own.
    - ❏ c. with partners.

6 B   The McGuffey Readers

The McGuffey Readers were textbooks that were used in schools in the United States in the nineteenth century. These were books of stories, poems, speeches, and essays. The readings were happy in tone so they would appeal to children. William McGuffey developed the books. He was a teacher from Ohio. The books were used to teach reading, writing, and spelling. They also taught moral values. The readings stressed honesty, charity, and hard work. These values often stayed with students long after they had grown up.

There were seven books in all. Each one was on a different reading level. Students began with the first book. It was called *The Eclectic First Reader for Young Children*. The word *eclectic* refers to the mix of stories and poems. When a student finished one book, he or she began the next. Students read the books at their own speed. A twelve-year-old and an eight-year-old might be on the same book. A student could graduate from school when he or she had read all the books.

The books had charts that showed how to say basic sounds. There was a list of new words at the start of each lesson. The books were illustrated with pictures.

The McGuffey Readers were first published in 1836. Although not used in today's schools, they are still available.

1. **Recognizing Words in Context**

   Find the word *appeal* in the passage. One definition below is closest to the meaning of that word. One definition has the opposite or nearly the opposite meaning. The remaining definition has a completely different meaning. Label the definitions C for *closest*, O for *opposite or nearly opposite*, and D for *different*.

   _____ a. interest

   _____ b. bore

   _____ c. grant

2. **Distinguishing Fact from Opinion**

   Two of the statements below present *facts*, which can be proved. The other statement is an *opinion*, which expresses someone's thoughts or beliefs. Label the statements F for *fact* and O for *opinion*.

   _____ a. There should have been eight levels of McGuffey Readers.

   _____ b. The McGuffey Readers had stories and poems in them.

   _____ c. William McGuffey was a teacher from Ohio.

3. Keeping Events in Order

Number the statements below 1, 2, and 3 to show the order in which the events took place.

_____ a. The McGuffey Readers are still available today.

_____ b. William McGuffey wrote the McGuffey Readers.

_____ c. Students used the books to learn to read and spell.

4. Making Correct Inferences

Two of the statements below are correct *inferences,* or reasonable guesses. They are based on information in the passage. The other statement is an incorrect, or faulty, inference. Label the statements C for *correct* inference and F for *faulty* inference.

_____ a. McGuffey's readers affected the way people behaved.

_____ b. Each of the McGuffey Readers continued the story started in the first book.

_____ c. A student studying the fifth McGuffey reader could probably read better than a student studying the third McGuffey reader.

5. Understanding Main Ideas

One of the statements below expresses the main idea of the passage. One statement is too general, or too broad. The other explains only part of the passage; it is too narrow. Label the statements M for *main idea,* B for *too broad,* and N for *too narrow.*

_____ a. Textbooks have been used in schools for a long time.

_____ b. The first reader was called *The Eclectic First Reader for Young Children.*

_____ c. The McGuffey Readers taught nineteenth-century schoolchildren to read and spell.

Correct Answers, Part A _____

Correct Answers, Part B _____

Total Correct Answers _____

The Kimono: Traditional Dress of Japan

The word *kimono* refers to traditional Japanese dress. The word comes from *kiru* (which means "to wear") and *mono* (which means "thing"). Men, women, and children all wear kimonos.

The basic kimono is a robe that hangs from the shoulders to the heels. It has square-cut sleeves and an open front that overlaps. All adult robes are made from one long, narrow length of fabric. The fabric width is not cut. It is sewn with wide or narrow seams to fit the wearer's shape. More than one robe may be worn at the same time.

The color, pattern, fabric, sleeve length, and sleeve shape depend on the wearer, the season, and the occasion. Women's sleeves are rounded. Men's sleeves are straight. Young girls wear bright colors and quite long sleeves. Unmarried women wear kimonos with large brightly colored designs and long sleeves. A bride may wear a white under-kimono and an over-kimono with a colored design. Some brides wear a set of four robes. Married women wear darker colors and shorter sleeves. Older women wear very dark colors and shorter sleeves. Men wear dark robes with a faint pattern or thin stripes. The most formal robes are made of silk and have five family crests, called *mon*. Less formal robes may have three *mon*. The most informal robes are cotton. They are worn in summer.

A kimono is closed with a sash, called an obi. Men's obi are narrow and plain. They wrap around the body and tie in the back. Women's obi come in many lengths, widths, colors, and designs. They tie in the back with a special bow. Extra pieces are needed to tie the sash. These give it volume, make it lay flat, and help it keep its shape.

A formal kimono for a woman may have 10 pieces. She may need help to dress. A formal outfit for a man includes a *hakama* (skirt-trouser) and a *haori* (short jacket). These are worn over the kimono. Women may also wear these pieces, but they never wear both at the same time.

Formal kimonos are worn with zori. These sandals have a thong that divides the big toe from the rest of the toes. They are worn with split-toe socks called *tabi*.

Today kimonos are usually worn only at special times. While at work or play, most Japanese wear western-style clothes.

Reading Time _____

Recalling Facts

1. The basic kimono is a
   - ❏ a. short jacket.
   - ❏ b. robe that hangs from the shoulders to the heels.
   - ❏ c. *hakama* and a *haori,* worn by both men and women.

2. All adult robes are made from
   - ❏ a. cotton.
   - ❏ b. one long, narrow length of fabric.
   - ❏ c. dark patterned fabric with a layer of thin stripes.

3. A kimono is closed by a sash called
   - ❏ a. an obi.
   - ❏ b. a *haori.*
   - ❏ c. a *hakama.*

4. *Tabi* are
   - ❏ a. formal robes.
   - ❏ b. pleated pants.
   - ❏ c. split-toe socks.

5. For work and play, most Japanese today wear
   - ❏ a. zori.
   - ❏ b. western-style clothes.
   - ❏ c. silk kimonos that have the five family crests.

Understanding Ideas

6. Which of the following sentences best tells what the whole passage is about?
   - ❏ a. The most formal kimonos have five *mon.*
   - ❏ b. A kimono is the traditional Japanese dress that is worn on special occasions.
   - ❏ c. The kind of clothes people wear can vary according to culture and beliefs.

7. A family would probably wear
   - ❏ a. matching kimonos.
   - ❏ b. a variety of kimonos.
   - ❏ c. obi of the same design.

8. The same type of kimono would usually be worn by
   - ❏ a. a bride and an older woman.
   - ❏ b. a young girl and her grand-mother.
   - ❏ c. a tall, thin woman and a short, heavy woman.

9. A person in a dark straight-sleeved kimono is most likely
   - ❏ a. a man.
   - ❏ b. a young girl.
   - ❏ c. an older woman.

10. From the passage, one can infer that formal kimonos are
    - ❏ a. worn often.
    - ❏ b. simple garments.
    - ❏ c. difficult to put on.

7 B Shichi-go-san: The Festival Day for Children in Japan

Shichi-go-san is Japanese for "seven, five, three." Shichi-go-san is a special day for boys ages three and five and girls ages three and seven. On November 15, parents take children of these ages to a shrine. There a priest says prayers for their healthy growth. Children wear ceremonial dress on this day. Before they go to the shrine, girls dress in kimonos. Boys dress in *haori* jackets and *hakama* pants. After prayers at the shrine, parents buy their children longevity candy. This shows that they wish for their children to live a long, long time. The candy is called *chitose-ame*, which means "1,000 years." It is made in long sticks that are red and white. It comes in a long bag with pictures of cranes and turtles. These animals are also the sign of long life.

The day has its roots in medieval times. Important families held rites as children grew. Up to age three, children's heads were kept shaved. At three, the hair was left to grow. At age five, boys first put on *hakama* pants. At age seven, girls first used obi to tie their kimonos. Then, in later years, all classes of families took their children to shrines.

1. **Recognizing Words in Context**

   Find the word *ceremonial* in the passage. One definition below is closest to the meaning of that word. One definition has the opposite or nearly the opposite meaning. The remaining definition has a completely different meaning. Label the definitions C for *closest*, O for *opposite or nearly opposite*, and D for *different*.

   _____ a. black

   _____ b. special

   _____ c. ordinary

2. **Distinguishing Fact from Opinion**

   Two of the statements below present *facts*, which can be proved. The other statement is an *opinion*, which expresses someone's thoughts or beliefs. Label the statements F for *fact* and O for *opinion*.

   _____ a. *Chitose-ame* is very tasty.

   _____ b. *Shichi-go-san* is on November 15.

   _____ c. *Shichi-go-san* is Japanese for "seven, five, three."

3. Keeping Events in Order

Number the statements below 1, 2, and 3 to show the order in which the events took place.

_____ a. The parents buy their children longevity candy.

_____ b. A priest says prayers for the children's healthy growth.

_____ c. The girls dress in kimonos and boys dress in *haori* jackets and *hakama* pants.

4. Making Correct Inferences

Two of the statements below are correct *inferences,* or reasonable guesses. They are based on information in the passage. The other statement is an incorrect, or faulty, inference. Label the statements C for *correct* inference and F for *faulty* inference.

_____ a. To see beautiful ceremonial clothes while in Japan, visit a shrine on November 15.

_____ b. The main purpose of *Shichi-go-san* is to celebrate Japanese ceremonial dress.

_____ c. *Shichi-go-san* is a very old tradition.

5. Understanding Main Ideas

One of the statements below expresses the main idea of the passage. One statement is too general, or too broad. The other explains only part of the passage; it is too narrow. Label the statements M for *main idea,* B for *too broad,* and N for *too narrow.*

_____ a. *Shichi-go-san* has its roots in medieval times.

_____ b. *Shichi-go-san* is one of many festivals that are celebrated in Japan.

_____ c. *Shichi-go-san* is a festival when priests pray for the healthy growth of the children.

Correct Answers, Part A _____

Correct Answers, Part B _____

Total Correct Answers _____

A region is an area that has similar features. These features make the region different from other areas. A region may have similar culture, history, or climate. It may have similar landforms, such as hills, valleys, or plains. It may have a similar function—that is, it may have many large cities or a lot of farmland. There are no set boundaries for regions. Sometimes the United States is divided up into five very large regions. These regions are the Northeast, Southeast, Midwest, Southwest, and West.

The Northeast region includes the area from Maine to Maryland and from the Atlantic Ocean to Pennsylvania. Near the ocean is a flat strip of land called a coastal plain. Most of the big cities are found there. Fishing is important to this area. The region is known for its seafood. Inland are the Appalachian Mountains. The climate of the Northeast has four seasons.

The Appalachian Mountains continue through the Southeast region. These mountains are rich in coal. This region spreads south through Florida and west through Arkansas. The coastal plains are near the ocean. In the south are the swamps of the Everglades. The Southeast climate is warm. There is a long season for growing crops.

The Midwest is flat and good for farming. Some Midwest states are near the Great Lakes. They have big cities and big industries. The other states are on the plains. The Central Plains get plenty of rain. Much corn is grown there. The Great Plains are drier. Wheat grows there. The Midwest has a climate with four seasons.

The Southwest shares a border with Mexico. The climate is dry. There are deserts, mountains, and canyons. It is warm in the deserts and cold in the mountains. The Four Corners region is where four states meet. They are Arizona, New Mexico, Utah, and Colorado.

Alaska and Hawaii are two states in the West. The rest of the states in the West are in two groups. The Mountain States have the Rocky Mountains. Winters there are long and cold. The Pacific States lie next to the Pacific Ocean. The Central Valley of California has rich farmland. It is warm there, and crops are grown year round. In the northwest part of this region, it can be warm but wet. There are rain forests with very tall trees. Lumber and wood products come from the West.

Reading Time _____

Recalling Facts

1. A region
   - ❏ a. covers a whole continent.
   - ❏ b. is a lot like the regions next to it.
   - ❏ c. has common features that make it different from other areas.

2. The Appalachian Mountains of the Southeast
   - ❏ a. are rich in coal.
   - ❏ b. have big cities and industry.
   - ❏ c. have a flat strip called a coastal plain.

3. The Central Plains and the Great Plains are in the
   - ❏ a. West.
   - ❏ b. Midwest.
   - ❏ c. Southwest.

4. Two states in the West are
   - ❏ a. Alaska and Hawaii.
   - ❏ b. Maine and Maryland.
   - ❏ c. Arizona and Alabama.

5. The Central Valley of California has
   - ❏ a. rain forests.
   - ❏ b. rich farmland.
   - ❏ c. the Rocky Mountains.

Understanding Ideas

6. From the passage, one can infer that
   - ❏ a. each state is a region.
   - ❏ b. people can have different ideas of regional boundaries.
   - ❏ c. Western regions are always larger than Eastern regions.

7. One would be least likely to find tall mountains in the
   - ❏ a. Midwest.
   - ❏ b. Northeast.
   - ❏ c. Southwest.

8. Of the following pairs, the regions with the most similar climates are the
   - ❏ a. Northeast and Midwest.
   - ❏ b. Midwest and Southeast.
   - ❏ c. Northeast and Southwest.

9. If a family wanted to see cactus plants in the desert, they would most likely visit the
   - ❏ a. Northeast.
   - ❏ b. Midwest.
   - ❏ c. Southwest.

10. Of the following, the region that has the greatest differences in climate from state to state is the
    - ❏ a. West.
    - ❏ b. Midwest.
    - ❏ c. Southeast.

8   B   The Rocky Mountain Region of the United States

Parts of Montana, Idaho, Wyoming, Utah, and Colorado have high, rugged mountain ranges. These ranges are all part of the Rocky Mountains. The Rockies were formed millions of years ago as pressure heaved up Earth's crust. Water running down the peaks carved out deep canyons. Later, glaciers shaped sharp peaks and broad valleys. Today there are still permanent ice caps on some peaks. The mountains are rich in minerals. Coal, copper, gold, iron ore, lead, and silver are mined here. The valleys are home to cattle and sheep ranches. The mountains are home to many kinds of wildlife. Elk, bears, moose, deer, beavers, and mountain goats live here. Lumber is cut from mountain forests.

The region has long cold winters and short summers. As one climbs a mountain, the temperature becomes colder. In this region, there are few cities. The small population is sparse, or spread out. Tourists come to the region in winter to ski. They come in summer to climb, hike, fish, camp, and raft on rushing rivers. The region has several parks. One of these is Yellowstone National Park. Here visitors can see geysers and hot springs. These are the result of a live volcano. Almost half of the park lies in a crater formed from an eruption.

1. Recognizing Words in Context

Find the word *sparse* in the passage. One definition below is closest to the meaning of that word. One definition has the opposite or nearly the opposite meaning. The remaining definition has a completely different meaning. Label the definitions C for *closest*, O for *opposite or nearly opposite*, and D for *different*.

_____ a. thin

_____ b. dense

_____ c. modern

2. Distinguishing Fact from Opinion

Two of the statements below present *facts*, which can be proved. The other statement is an *opinion*, which expresses someone's thoughts or beliefs. Label the statements F for *fact* and O for *opinion*.

_____ a. The Rockies were formed millions of years ago.

_____ b. The region has long cold winters and short summers.

_____ c. The Rocky Mountain region is the most beautiful place on Earth.

3. Keeping Events in Order

Number the statements below 1, 2, and 3 to show the order in which the events took place.

_____ a. Glaciers shaped sharp peaks and broad valleys.

_____ b. There are still permanent ice caps on some peaks.

_____ c. The mountains were formed as pressure heaved up Earth's crust.

4. Making Correct Inferences

Two of the statements below are correct *inferences,* or reasonable guesses. They are based on information in the passage. The other statement is an incorrect, or faulty, inference. Label the statements C for *correct* inference and F for *faulty* inference.

_____ a. Most of the region lies in Yellowstone Park.

_____ b. Much of the Rocky Mountain region is wilderness.

_____ c. There are many activities for tourists in the Rockies.

5. Understanding Main Ideas

One of the statements below expresses the main idea of the passage. One statement is too general, or too broad. The other explains only part of the passage; it is too narrow. Label the statements M for *main idea,* B for *too broad,* and N for *too narrow.*

_____ a. The Rocky Mountain region has few cities, and the population is sparse.

_____ b. The Rocky Mountains are just one of the many mountainous regions in the United States.

_____ c. The rugged Rocky Mountain region has a cold climate, a small population, and many natural resources.

Correct Answers, Part A _____

Correct Answers, Part B _____

Total Correct Answers _____

How Does Folklore Help Us Learn about the Past?

Every culture has its own folklore. These tales and bits of wisdom teach children how to behave and what to believe. Folklore includes legends, songs, art, tales, myths, and proverbs. It is handed down from one generation to the next.

Folklore helps keep history alive. Legends are folktales that are based on true stories. But the plain truth about history is not always exciting. So the storyteller invents details to keep the listener's interest. The tale becomes so interesting that it gets retold. Thus, a legend is born. One such legend is about Davy Crockett. Davy Crockett lived in the backwoods of the frontier. He became a statesman, and he fought in a war with Mexico. His brave deeds were exaggerated in stories. He came to stand for the spirit of the frontier. Children loved the tales. They learned about frontier life through stories about Davy Crockett.

Tall tales are folktales that stretch the truth. They are sometimes told to fool those who hear them. There are many tall tales of the American West. An example of a tall tale is the story about Paul Bunyan, the giant lumberjack. It is said that his clothes were so large that his shirt buttons were wagon wheels. Tales about Bunyan are set at his lumber camp. The tales are fun to hear. They also show what life was like in a lumber camp.

Myths are folktales that tell how the universe was made. They tell where the first humans came from. Myths are about gods or divine beings in human or animal form. People who told myths thought the stories were true—and so did the listeners. Myths can teach us about people's beliefs and values.

Fairy tales may also tell us more about a culture. These folktales are not believed by the teller or by the audience. They are tales such as "Snow White" or "The Three Little Pigs." They often begin with the words "Once upon a time . . ." The same tale may exist in different forms in more than one culture.

Studying folklore is one way to learn about a culture. People who study folklore are called folklorists. Folklorists look at more than just folktales. They look at folk art, folk music, poetry, and proverbs. A proverb is a wise saying such as "The early bird gets the worm." Proverbs are used to teach children the wisdom of their elders.

Reading Time _____

Recalling Facts

1. Folklore teaches children
   - ❏ a. how to talk.
   - ❏ b. what will happen the future.
   - ❏ c. how to behave and what to believe.

2. The tale of Davy Crockett is a
   - ❏ a. myth.
   - ❏ b. legend.
   - ❏ c. proverb.

3. Tall tales are stories that
   - ❏ a. exaggerate or stretch the truth.
   - ❏ b. tell about the first humans on Earth.
   - ❏ c. tell about divine beings in human or animal form.

4. People who study folklore are called
   - ❏ a. folklorists.
   - ❏ b. storytellers.
   - ❏ c. mythologists.

5. A proverb is a
   - ❏ a. song.
   - ❏ b. wise saying.
   - ❏ c. long, exaggerated poem.

Understanding Ideas

6. Folklore is least likely to teach children
   - ❏ a. how to ride a bike.
   - ❏ b. that it is important to be honest.
   - ❏ c. when to say "please" and "thank you."

7. From the passage, one can infer that
   - ❏ a. another word for *folklore* is *myth*.
   - ❏ b. there are many kinds of folklore.
   - ❏ c. cultures always share the same myths.

8. Of the following, a folklorist is most likely to be interested in
   - ❏ a. a court decision.
   - ❏ b. jump rope rhymes.
   - ❏ c. newspaper headlines.

9. "Cinderella" is most likely a
   - ❏ a. myth.
   - ❏ b. legend.
   - ❏ c. fairy tale.

10. One can infer from the passage that a tall tale is
    - ❏ a. all truth.
    - ❏ b. all fiction.
    - ❏ c. both truth and fiction.

9   B   Johnny Appleseed: The Man and the Legend

John Chapman was born in Massachusetts about 1774. He grew up to be a gardener. He planted apple trees in New York and Pennsylvania. In the early 1800s, he carried apple seeds west. He walked the wilderness that would later become Michigan, Ohio, Indiana, and Illinois. When he found a good place for apple trees, he cleared the brush. He planted the seeds in rows. Then he fenced them in. At first he went back east for more seeds. Later he got seeds from the trees he grew. He roamed through the wilderness, tending to his orchards. He traveled on foot, often without shoes. He carried with him a cooking pot.

When the first settlers came, Chapman sold his trees for pennies. Sometimes he traded them for used clothes. The settlers called him Johnny Appleseed. Those who moved on west told of the man who sold them the trees. The tale passed down through the generations. More tales were added to the legend. In one tale, Johnny Appleseed slept through a storm with a bear. In another, a rattlesnake tried to bite his foot, but his skin was too tough. In books, he might be shown in clothes that are too big, wearing his pot as a hat. Some of the trees he planted still bear fruit today.

1. **Recognizing Words in Context**

   Find the word *roamed* in the passage. One definition below is closest to the meaning of that word. One definition has the opposite or nearly the opposite meaning. The remaining definition has a completely different meaning. Label the definitions C for *closest*, O for *opposite or nearly opposite*, and D for *different*.

   _____ a. drove

   _____ b. stayed

   _____ c. wandered

2. **Distinguishing Fact from Opinion**

   Two of the statements below present *facts*, which can be proved. The other statement is an *opinion*, which expresses someone's thoughts or beliefs. Label the statements F for *fact* and O for *opinion*.

   _____ a. Chapman sold trees to settlers.

   _____ b. Chapman was born in Massachusetts.

   _____ c. Johnny Appleseed is the best folktale.

3. Keeping Events in Order

Number the statements below 1, 2, and 3 to show the order in which the events took place.

_____ a. Chapman cleared the brush.

_____ b. Chapman fenced the trees in.

_____ c. Chapman planted the seeds in rows.

4. Making Correct Inferences

Two of the statements below are correct *inferences,* or reasonable guesses. They are based on information in the passage. The other statement is an incorrect, or faulty, inference. Label the statements C for *correct* inference and F for *faulty* inference.

_____ a. Chapman planted many apple orchards in several states.

_____ b. Chapman was a colorful character that people remembered.

_____ c. All of the apple trees in the United States today are a result of Chapman's work.

5. Understanding Main Ideas

One of the statements below expresses the main idea of the passage. One statement is too general, or too broad. The other explains only part of the passage; it is too narrow. Label the statements M for *main idea,* B for *too broad,* and N for *too narrow.*

_____ a. Johnny Appleseed carried a cooking pot.

_____ b. Johnny Appleseed became one of the many frontier legends.

_____ c. Johnny Appleseed was a real man who planted apple trees and inspired a legend.

Correct Answers, Part A _____

Correct Answers, Part B _____

Total Correct Answers _____

El Pueblo: The Birthplace of the City of Angels

In the late eighteenth century, Spain ruled Mexico. California also belonged to Spain. It was a vast place with scattered native tribes and a few Spanish missions. Britain and Russia tried to move in on the land. Felipe de Neve was California's governor. He thought a new town might help solve the problem. It would improve Spain's claim to the land. Food could be grown there for Spain's troops. Up to that time, food had to be brought in by ship. De Neve chose a site on a low plain. It was by the ocean and on the Los Angeles River.

Finding settlers for the new town was a problem. People did not want to go there, even for free land and livestock. The search for settlers took months. At last, de Neve found 12 families. They were Native Americans, Africans, Spaniards, and people of mixed race. In 1781 they reached the site. They named it El Pueblo de la Reina de Los Angeles. The name means "the Town of the Queen of the Angels."

In the first years, they built a plaza, or town square. Buildings were made of sun-dried brick, called adobe. Land grants were given to soldiers. Cattle was raised on the first ranches. The first orange grove in California was planted. At about this time, California was split—Baja was in the south, and Alta was in the north. El Pueblo was part of Alta.

In 1821 Mexico broke free of Spain. The new governors gave more land grants in Alta to new settlers. Some of these settlers came by ship from the East Coast or from Europe. More came by wagon train. They started businesses and ranches. In 1846 the United States went to war with Mexico. After the war, Alta became the state of California. When gold was found in California, El Pueblo sold food to the miners.

For the next 30 years, the people of Los Angeles kept their Mexican traditions. Spanish was still the main language. This changed as people from other cultures came. The railroad opened new markets for trade. It also brought more people. Numbers of Chinese, French, and Italian settlers came. Later the movie business came to the city. During World War II, the city's factories made things needed for the war. Workers came for jobs. Farms were turned into suburbs. Today Los Angeles is the second-largest city in the United States.

Reading Time _____

Recalling Facts

1. In the eighteenth century, Mexico was ruled by
   - ❑ a. Spain.
   - ❑ b. France.
   - ❑ c. the United States.

2. Felipe de Neve wanted to start a new town because
   - ❑ a. he wanted a town to be named for him.
   - ❑ b. it would improve Spain's claim to the land.
   - ❑ c. he wanted to bring religion to the Native American people.

3. People did not want to settle in the new town because the land was too
   - ❑ a. rocky.
   - ❑ b. remote.
   - ❑ c. expensive.

4. *El Pueblo* means
   - ❑ a. the town.
   - ❑ b. big house.
   - ❑ c. the harbor.

5. Today Los Angeles is the _____ city in the nation.
   - ❑ a. largest
   - ❑ b. second-largest
   - ❑ c. seventh-largest

Understanding Ideas

6. Which of the following sentences best tells what the whole passage is about?
   - ❑ a. El Pueblo was part of Alta California.
   - ❑ b. Felipe de Neve started the town of El Pueblo.
   - ❑ c. Los Angeles grew from a Spanish pueblo to a very large city.

7. From the passage, one can infer that non-Mexican newcomers
   - ❑ a. became part of the Mexican culture of El Pueblo.
   - ❑ b. brought their own languages and cultures with them.
   - ❑ c. adopted the Spanish language and gave up their own languages.

8. The growth of Los Angeles shows that
   - ❑ a. all towns grow larger.
   - ❑ b. de Neve chose a good site for the town.
   - ❑ c. without the Gold Rush, Los Angeles would not be a city today.

9. From the passage, one can infer that Baja California is now
   - ❑ a. part of Mexico.
   - ❑ b. a state in the United States.
   - ❑ c. ruled by Spain.

10. One can infer that Los Angeles
    - ❑ a. has not changed much throughout its history.
    - ❑ b. is mostly populated by descendants of the first settlers.
    - ❑ c. has drawn people from across the United States and from around the world.

A Visit to Olvera Street

In 1926 Christine Sterling took a walk through the plaza in the oldest part of Los Angeles. The area was run-down and shabby. On a small lane stood a few rooms of a condemned house. The lane was Olvera Street. It had been named for Agustin Olvera, who had once lived there. He was the first county judge of Los Angeles. The old house was the Avila Adobe. It had been one of the finest houses in the city. The city's mayor had lived there. Sterling was sad that the birthplace of Los Angeles had become so run-down. She started a corporation to raise funds to fix it up. The *Los Angeles Times* told of the project. Many people gave money. The city drew the plans to fix the street. Prisoners did some of the work. Other people also gave their time and labor.

Today Olvera Street is a Mexican marketplace. It is lined with stores and wood stalls. Tourists come to shop for handmade pots, toys, clothes, art, and jewelry. Musicians stroll up and down the street playing instruments. Native peoples dance. One can eat Mexican food and visit the Avila Adobe. The street is part of a large state park. The park includes the plaza, or town square, and many restored buildings.

1. Recognizing Words in Context

Find the word *shabby* in the passage. One definition below is closest to the meaning of that word. One definition has the opposite or nearly the opposite meaning. The remaining definition has a completely different meaning. Label the definitions C for *closest*, O for *opposite or nearly opposite*, and D for *different*.

_____ a. neat

_____ b. quiet

_____ c. neglected

2. Distinguishing Fact from Opinion

Two of the statements below present *facts*, which can be proved. The other statement is an *opinion*, which expresses someone's thoughts or beliefs. Label the statements F for *fact* and O for *opinion*.

_____ a. Olvera Street was named for Agustin Olvera.

_____ b. Today Olvera Street is a Mexican marketplace.

_____ c. Olvera Street is the most interesting place to visit in all of Los Angeles.

3. Keeping Events in Order

Number the statements below 1, 2, and 3 to show the order in which the events took place.

_____ a. Sterling started a corporation to raise funds to fix it up.

_____ b. In 1926 Sterling took a walk through the oldest part of Los Angeles.

_____ c. Sterling was sad to see that the birthplace of Los Angeles was so run-down.

4. Making Correct Inferences

Two of the statements below are correct *inferences,* or reasonable guesses. They are based on information in the passage. The other statement is an incorrect, or faulty, inference. Label the statements C for *correct* inference and F for *faulty* inference.

_____ a. Today the birthplace of Los Angeles is alive and celebrates its past.

_____ b. Sterling wanted to fix up Olvera Street so that she could live in the finest house in the city.

_____ c. Sterling's dream of fixing up Olvera Street was the beginning of a larger project that became a historic park.

5. Understanding Main Ideas

One of the statements below expresses the main idea of the passage. One statement is too general, or too broad. The other explains only part of the passage; it is too narrow. Label the statements M for *main idea*, B for *too broad*, and N for *too narrow*.

_____ a. Christine Sterling raised funds to help Olvera Street become a Mexican marketplace so that it could be a reminder of the city's history.

_____ b. On Olvera Street, one can shop for Mexican pottery, toys, clothes, art, and jewelry.

_____ c. It is important to repair historic landmarks, such as Olvera Street.

Correct Answers, Part A _____

Correct Answers, Part B _____

Total Correct Answers _____

The Continental Army: America's First Army

By 1775 many American colonists wanted to be free of British rule. These patriots had gathered arms and formed troops. They could be ready to fight quickly, so they were called Minutemen. In New England, these groups formed armies to protect their regions. In the spring, the Second Continental Congress met. John Adams thought the colonies needed a grand army to defend themselves. Congress agreed to take on the expense of a united army. George Washington was chosen to lead the troops.

That summer Washington took charge of the Continental Army. There were about 17,000 soldiers. They were not well trained. Soldiers signed up for a few weeks and then went home. There were shortages of gunpowder, horses, and uniforms. Some people, including some members of Congress, did not support the army. They feared it would rule the country after the war. This made it hard for the army to get supplies. Washington did the best he could with what he had. Some soldiers wore parts of old uniforms. The rest wore their own clothes. Badges were worn to show rank.

The British soldiers were well trained. They had tents, food, guns, and red uniforms. The British also had funds to hire troops to fight with them. Some of these mercenaries were the German Hessians. Still, the Continental Army had some advantages. The colonists knew the land well. They could hide and launch surprise attacks. They could quickly call up more men. Most of all, they were fighting for their freedom.

In the fall of 1776, the British took over New York City. Washington's small army of three thousand men retreated across the Delaware River. The British thought they had won the war. In a bold move on Christmas Day, Washington and his men crossed the river at night. Their password was "Victory or Death!" They surprised the Hessian troops, who gave up. This did much to boost the morale of the army.

By the winter of 1777, the army was in sad shape. The soldiers were camped at Valley Forge. They lacked tents and food. It was cold and some men did not have shoes. More than two thousand died. Baron von Steuben, a military leader from Prussia, joined them. He trained and drilled the troops. They became a strong fighting force. In 1778 France joined the colonies in the war. Their guns, soldiers, and ships helped the Continental Army win the war.

Reading Time _____

Recalling Facts

1. In 1775 colonists who wanted to be free of British rule were called
   - ❏ a. patriots.
   - ❏ b. redcoats.
   - ❏ c. Hessians.

2. When Washington took charge of the Continental Army, the soldiers
   - ❏ a. needed training.
   - ❏ b. were well trained to fight a war.
   - ❏ c. had the most up-to-date supplies.

3. When Washington took charge of the army, the soldiers wore _____ to show their ranks.
   - ❏ a. hats
   - ❏ b. badges
   - ❏ c. uniforms

4. One strength of the Continental Army was
   - ❏ a. mercenaries.
   - ❏ b. knowledge of the land.
   - ❏ c. a good supply of tents, food, guns, and uniforms.

5. In 1778 the colonies were joined in the war by
   - ❏ a. France.
   - ❏ b. Canada.
   - ❏ c. Germany.

Understanding Ideas

6. Which sentence best tells what the whole passage is about?
   - ❏ a. Washington took charge of almost 17,000 soldiers in the Continental Army.
   - ❏ b. Washington led the Continental Army to victory over the British even though the army had many disadvantages.
   - ❏ c. The Continental Army was formed in 1775 because a grand army was needed to protect the colonies.

7. It probably took more time to call up British soldiers because
   - ❏ a. Great Britain was smaller than America.
   - ❏ b. British soldiers were afraid of the patriots.
   - ❏ c. they had to come by sea from Great Britain.

8. Most soldiers likely stayed at Valley Forge because they
   - ❏ a. had signed up.
   - ❏ b. believed in their cause.
   - ❏ c. were paid well for their duties as soldiers.

9. From the passage, one can infer that George Washington was
   - ❏ a. a poor leader.
   - ❏ b. defeated by the British.
   - ❏ c. an inspiration to his soldiers.

10. From the passage, one can infer that the Continental Army had
    - ❏ a. great hardships.
    - ❏ b. little trouble winning a war against the British.
    - ❏ c. much more military experience than the British.

11 B   Who Were the Soldiers in the Continental Army?

The soldiers of the Continental Army were the rich and the poor. They were farmers, blacksmiths, merchants, and woodsmen. They were boys and men of all ages. Many had to learn how to carry, load, and shoot a rifle. Most knew nothing about fighting. A few were Native Americans. Some were African Americans, both free and enslaved. One enslaved man who fought was Peter Salem. He killed a British leader at the Battle of Bunker Hill. At one time, Congress did not allow enslaved persons in the army. Salem's owners freed him so he could stay in the army. Some women traveled with the army. They cooked and mended clothes. They nursed the sick and fought in combat.

These people came together to fight for one goal—freedom. Many endured hardships. "Long Bill" Scott was one of these freedom fighters. He was captured by the British in Boston. He escaped and rejoined the army in New York. Then he was captured in New York and escaped again. But "Long Bill" Scott was determined to fight for his country. When he rejoined the army, he brought his sons and some other men that he had recruited. He was wounded nine times. He had to sell his farm to pay his war expenses. He suffered through all of this to fight for freedom.

1. **Recognizing Words in Context**

   Find the word *endured* in the passage. One definition below is closest to the meaning of that word. One definition has the opposite or nearly the opposite meaning. The remaining definition has a completely different meaning. Label the definitions C for *closest*, O for *opposite or nearly opposite*, and D for *different*.

   _____ a. gave in

   _____ b. suffered

   _____ c. increased

2. **Distinguishing Fact from Opinion**

   Two of the statements below present *facts*, which can be proved. The other statement is an *opinion*, which expresses someone's thoughts or beliefs. Label the statements F for *fact* and O for *opinion*.

   _____ a. "Long Bill" Scott was wounded nine times.

   _____ b. "Long Bill" Scott was the most famous person in the army.

   _____ c. Peter Salem was an enslaved African American who fought in the Continental Army.

3. Keeping Events in Order

Number the statements below 1, 2, and 3 to show the order in which the events took place.

_____ a. Scott was captured by the British in Boston.

_____ b. After Scott escaped, he rejoined the army in New York.

_____ c. Scott was captured in New York, but he escaped again.

4. Making Correct Inferences

Two of the statements below are correct *inferences*, or reasonable guesses. They are based on information in the passage. The other statement is an incorrect, or faulty, inference. Label the statements C for *correct* inference and F for *faulty* inference.

_____ a. The only women who traveled with the army were nurses.

_____ b. The soldiers of the Continental Army were from all walks of life.

_____ c. "Long Bill" Scott was very committed to the cause of the Revolutionary War.

5. Understanding Main Ideas

One of the statements below expresses the main idea of the passage. One statement is too general, or too broad. The other explains only part of the passage; it is too narrow. Label the statements M for *main idea*, B for *too broad*, and N for *too narrow*.

_____ a. The soldiers of the Continental Army were people of different ages, races, and classes who were united in their fight for freedom.

_____ b. The soldiers of the Continental Army fought the British in the Revolutionary War.

_____ c. At one time, Congress did not allow enslaved people in the army.

Correct Answers, Part A _____

Correct Answers, Part B _____

Total Correct Answers _____

12　A　The Nile River: Lifeblood of Ancient Egypt

The Nile is the world's longest river. It starts in the mountains of East Africa. It flows through the barren desert and ends in the Mediterranean Sea. Along its banks, the first great African civilization grew. This was ancient Egypt. By 5000 B.C., people were living on the Nile's floodplain. This lowland on both sides of the river floods once a year. Each spring, snowmelt in the mountains sends a rush of water down the river. The fast water picks up silt, which is bits of soil and plant matter. In the desert, the Nile overflows its banks. When the water recedes, it leaves a layer of silt. This rich new topsoil is good for growing crops. When the crops are growing, the land near the river looks like a green ribbon running through the brown desert. The long Nile valley is only five miles wide in some places.

The ancient people planted their seeds in the mud. They grew wheat, barley, flax, beans, chickpeas, onions, and other vegetables. They also grew trees that produced fruit, such as figs and dates. Because the climate is warm, there is a long growing season. Two or three crops could be grown each year. The people built canals and basins that filled with water when the river flooded. They used this water on the crops for the rest of the year. A flood that had less water than normal meant there would be fewer crops that year.

Besides growing crops, the ancient people of the Nile gathered wild fruits, seeds, and roots near the river. They fished the river for catfish, perch, and other kinds of fish. Animals—such as gazelles, hyenas, and birds—lived on the river's banks. The people hunted these animals for food. They tamed other animals and kept them as livestock. They raised cattle and flocks of geese. From these animals, they got meat, eggs, and fat.

The Nile was more than a source of food to the ancient Egyptians. They dried and bundled the reeds that grew by the water. They coated the reeds with straw and mud and used them to build homes. They made roofs for their homes from the fronds of palm trees that grew by the water. They built their first monuments to their gods from sun-dried mud bricks. They traveled on the river in boats made from reeds and wood.

Reading Time _____

Recalling Facts

1. The first great African civilization grew
   - ❑ a. in the barren desert.
   - ❑ b. along the banks of the Nile.
   - ❑ c. in the mountains of East Africa.

2. The lowland on both sides of the Nile river that floods once a year is called the
   - ❑ a. canal.
   - ❑ b. wetland.
   - ❑ c. floodplain.

3. The people built canals and basins to catch the floodwaters so they could
   - ❑ a. attract wild animals.
   - ❑ b. water the crops the rest of the year.
   - ❑ c. store drinking water for the dry season.

4. At its narrowest, the Nile valley is _____ miles wide.
   - ❑ a. 5
   - ❑ b. 20
   - ❑ c. 30

5. The ancient Egyptians raised
   - ❑ a. hyenas and gazelles.
   - ❑ b. wild seeds and roots.
   - ❑ c. cattle and flocks of geese.

Understanding Ideas

6. From the passage, one can infer that the ancient Egyptians ate
   - ❑ a. mostly grains.
   - ❑ b. a variety of foods.
   - ❑ c. the same foods every day.

7. It is likely that Egypt is sometimes called "Gift of the Nile" because
   - ❑ a. it could not have existed without the river.
   - ❑ b. it began on the banks of the world's longest river.
   - ❑ c. the river gave the Egyptians a way to travel from place to place.

8. From the passage, one can infer that ancient civilizations grew
   - ❑ a. in desert areas.
   - ❑ b. where there were animals.
   - ❑ c. where there was a source of water.

9. In contrast to the African desert, the Nile valley is
   - ❑ a. drier.
   - ❑ b. greener.
   - ❑ c. a lot larger.

10. Which of the following sentences best tells what the whole passage is about?
   - ❑ a. The Nile River gave life to ancient Egypt.
   - ❑ b. Ancient people developed a great civilization in Egypt.
   - ❑ c. The ancient Egyptians grew crops on the Nile's floodplain.

　　　　The Boats of Ancient Egypt

The ancient Egyptians traveled most often by boat. The Nile River became a bustling freeway of boats, from simple rafts to beautiful boats.

Rafts and small boats were made of papyrus reeds. The ambatch was a small craft shaped like a canoe. To make an ambatch, a person first tied two bundles of reeds together at the ends. Then the reeds were parted in the middle to form the sides and the bottom of the boat. Finally, a reed mat was placed in the boat for a floor. A person would use a paddle to move the boat.

Large boats were made from wood. Boats called merchantmen carried trade goods. These boats had sails, but they were also rowed by many people. Large ships went down the Nile to the Mediterranean Sea.

Barges were large wooden boats pulled by smaller boats. Enslaved people rowed the smaller boats. Some barges carried animals. Others carried the blocks of stone used to build the pyramids. Kings rode on royal barges that were painted to tell a story. The king sat under a cloth cover. It is thought that Queen Cleopatra had a royal barge with private rooms. Funeral barges carried dead kings to their tombs. Solar barges were often buried near the kings. People thought the kings could use these boats in the afterlife.

1. **Recognizing Words in Context**

   Find the word *bustling* in the passage. One definition below is closest to the meaning of that word. One definition has the opposite or nearly the opposite meaning. The remaining definition has a completely different meaning. Label the definitions C for *closest,* O for *opposite or nearly opposite,* and D for *different.*

   _____ a. quiet

   _____ b. busy

   _____ c. open

2. **Distinguishing Fact from Opinion**

   Two of the statements below present *facts,* which can be proved. The other statement is an *opinion,* which expresses someone's thoughts or beliefs. Label the statements F for *fact* and O for *opinion.*

   _____ a. An ambatch was a small craft shaped like a canoe.

   _____ b. Boats called merchantmen carried trade goods.

   _____ c. Barges were better boats than ambatches.

3. Keeping Events in Order

Number the statements below 1, 2, and 3 to show the order in which the events took place.

_____ a. A reed mat was placed on the bottom for a floor.

_____ b. A person tied bundles of reeds together at the ends.

_____ c. The reeds were parted in the middle to form sides and a bottom.

4. Making Correct Inferences

Two of the statements below are correct *inferences,* or reasonable guesses. They are based on information in the passage. The other statement is an incorrect, or faulty, inference. Label the statements C for *correct* inference and F for *faulty* inference.

_____ a. The Egyptians had different boats for different uses.

_____ b. Egyptian kings traveled the Nile on solar barges.

_____ c. The royal barges were fancier than trade ships.

5. Understanding Main Ideas

One of the statements below expresses the main idea of the passage. One statement is too general, or too broad. The other explains only part of the passage; it is too narrow. Label the statements M for *main idea*, B for *too broad,* and N for *too narrow.*

_____ a. Smaller boats pulled barges on the Nile River.

_____ b. Through the ages, Egyptians have traveled the Nile by boat.

_____ c. The ancient Egyptians built boats of all kinds to transport people, animals, and goods on the Nile River.

Correct Answers, Part A _____

Correct Answers, Part B _____

Total Correct Answers _____

Entrepreneurs are people who start and run their own businesses. They want to be in control of their own time and fortune. They take the risk of investing in a business. If it succeeds, they make a profit. If it fails, they take the loss. Entrepreneurs work in a free enterprise system. This means that people can own resources such as land, computers, and buildings. They can use these to make goods or offer services. A business must follow certain laws. However, a business owner has the freedom to make most decisions.

How does a person know what kind of business to start? An entrepreneur sees a need that is not being filled. This is called an "opportunity niche." For example, many people in a small town have pets. The closest place to leave the pets while on vacation is 50 miles away. A pet-sitting service would fill this niche.

Entrepreneurs often invent new things. In the 1940s, George de Mestral took his dog for a walk. His pants picked up plant burrs. He looked at the burrs under a microscope. They had tiny hooks that stuck to the loops of the pants fabric. He thought of making a hook-and-loop fastener. Thus, Velcro was born.

Entrepreneurs may not have the funds to start a business. But that does not stop them. They may borrow money from a bank. They may convince others to invest in their ideas for a share of the profits. In New York, teen Jeffrey Rodriguez learned to paint with an airbrush. This is a tool that uses air to spray paint on a surface. His first tools were borrowed from his Boy Scout leader. His dad let him use a storefront that the family owned. Rodriguez and a partner, John Serrano, started a custom art business. They called it Latin Artist. Still, they needed money. Rodriguez learned of a group that gave grants to businesses that stressed community service. A grant is money that does not have to be paid back. Rodriguez and his partner won a grant. Latin Artist gives young people free art lessons. The grant was used to fix up their workshop.

Once a business is running, entrepreneurs can change course as they go. They can come back and try again after a loss. Some start one business after another. They apply what they learn to each new venture.

Reading Time _____

Recalling Facts

1. Entrepreneurs are people who
   - ❑ a. start and run businesses.
   - ❑ b. work for a friend's business.
   - ❑ c. help others make a profit from their businesses.

2. In a free enterprise system,
   - ❑ a. the government owns and operates all businesses.
   - ❑ b. someone owns resources and uses them to make goods or offer services.
   - ❑ c. resources are rented from the government, and businesses are run for a share of the profits.

3. An opportunity niche is
   - ❑ a. a need that is not being filled.
   - ❑ b. money to start a new business.
   - ❑ c. laws that a business must follow.

4. George de Mestral invented
   - ❑ a. Velcro.
   - ❑ b. the air brush.
   - ❑ c. community service.

5. A grant is
   - ❑ a. a business tax.
   - ❑ b. money that does not have to be paid back.
   - ❑ c. a loan that must be paid back within a year.

Understanding Ideas

6. Entrepreneurs need to be
   - ❑ a. creative and persistent.
   - ❑ b. willing to give up quickly.
   - ❑ c. able to start new businesses without any plans.

7. The most likely reason entrepreneurs take risks is that they
   - ❑ a. believe in their ideas.
   - ❑ b. are certain they will succeed.
   - ❑ c. need money and cannot get a bank loan.

8. Which one of the following may be an entrepreneur?
   - ❑ a. a store owner
   - ❑ b. a school teacher
   - ❑ c. a factory worker

9. Which of the following does *not* describe an opportunity niche?
   - ❑ a. a hot day and thirsty people
   - ❑ b. a large mall without a shoe store
   - ❑ c. a small town with six gas stations

10. Which of the following sentences best tells what the whole passage is about?
    - ❑ a. Entrepreneurs are often inventors.
    - ❑ b. Entrepreneurs start and run businesses based on their own creative ideas.
    - ❑ c. The United States has a free enterprise system.

13 B Steps for Starting a Business—for Young People

Step one: Decide what kind of business to start. A person who likes to be outside might mow lawns. A teen who baby-sits might start a day camp for children.

Step two: Make sure there is a need for the business. Neighbors who dislike lawn chores might pay to have them done. Mothers of small children might pay to send them to camp.

Step three: Answer the following question. How can the new business be better than businesses that are already out there? A new lawn care service might cut grass free every fourth time. A day camp for children might teach crafts.

Step four: Get the needed resources. A lawn care service needs a mower and other tools. A camp needs snacks, craft supplies, and a sheltered, shady space. It may need an indoor space too. Some resources may have to be purchased. An entrepreneur might borrow money to buy them.

Step five: Advertise. Give out flyers or place an ad in a local paper.

Step six: Do what is promised in the ads. People will go back often to a business they can rely on.

Step seven: Expand the business. When the money comes in, put some of it back into the business. This might mean purchasing better equipment. It could mean hiring workers to take on more customers.

1. **Recognizing Words in Context**

   Find the word *expand* in the passage. One definition below is closest to the meaning of that word. One definition has the opposite or nearly the opposite meaning. The remaining definition has a completely different meaning. Label the definitions C for *closest*, O for *opposite or nearly opposite*, and D for *different*.

   _____ a. shrink

   _____ b. explain

   _____ c. increase

2. **Distinguishing Fact from Opinion**

   Two of the statements below present *facts*, which can be proved. The other statement is an *opinion*, which expresses someone's thoughts or beliefs. Label the statements F for *fact* and O for *opinion*.

   _____ a. A children's camp is a better business for a teen than a lawn care service.

   _____ b. Entrepreneurs can borrow money to start a business.

   _____ c. A lawn care service needs a mower and other tools.

3. Keeping Events in Order

Number the statements below 1, 2, and 3 to show the order in which the events took place.

_____ a. Get the needed resources.

_____ b. Decide what kind of business to start.

_____ c. When the money comes in, put some of it back into the business.

4. Making Correct Inferences

Two of the statements below are correct *inferences*, or reasonable guesses. They are based on information in the passage. The other statement is an incorrect, or faulty, inference. Label the statements C for *correct* inference and F for *faulty* inference.

_____ a. Any business that is started will succeed.

_____ b. It takes careful planning and hard work to start and run a business.

_____ c. To earn money from a business, time and money must be invested.

5. Understanding Main Ideas

One of the statements below expresses the main idea of the passage. One statement is too general, or too broad. The other explains only part of the passage; it is too narrow. Label the statements M for *main idea*, B for *too broad*, and N for *too narrow*.

_____ a. Some resources may have to be purchased when starting a business.

_____ b. Young people can follow a series of steps to help them start a business.

_____ c. Businesses can be started by young people or adults.

Correct Answers, Part A _____

Correct Answers, Part B _____

Total Correct Answers _____

The Authority of the Kings and Queens of England

The United Kingdom (UK) of Great Britain and Northern Ireland is a constitutional monarchy. This means that a monarch (king or queen) is the head of state. His or her powers are limited by a constitution. These are laws and customs that serve as a framework for government. Laws are made by Parliament, which is made up of the House of Lords and the House of Commons. The members of the House of Lords are peers (nobles) and officials of the Church of England. The members of the House of Commons are elected, and they are paid. Members of Parliament have the real power to govern. The king or queen can advise Parliament and can name new peers.

In the sixth century, the first kings of England were warlords. They seized land by force and passed it down to their heirs. They led warriors who fought to keep the land. The warriors were the barons, or lords. For their service, the king gave them land and wealth. To get wealth, a king taxed the people. These first kings had the power to solve disputes. They could fine and punish people. They made the laws.

Parliament began as a group of lords. Their job was to advise the monarch. Later the lords fought with the kings and queens for power. In the thirteenth century, the lords forced King John to sign the Magna Carta. It stated that upper-class people had certain rights. For example, they could not be put in jail without a trial. It held that even the king must obey the law. Years later the barons forced the king to have a permanent council of barons. Baron Simon de Montfort called some of his knights to attend one meeting. They were commoners. From then on, commoners took part in Parliament.

In the fourteenth century, the king could not make new taxes without Parliament's consent. Parliament split into the House of Lords and the House of Commons. In the next century, the House of Commons gained the same powers as the House of Lords.

A war between Parliament and Charles I was fought in the seventeenth century. The king lost his throne. After the war, the Bill of Rights was written. It gave Parliament more power than the king or queen. Today the queen has little power. She often attends ceremonies, and she is respected by the people as a symbol of their country.

Reading Time _____

Recalling Facts

1. The United Kingdom of Great Britain and Northern Ireland is a
   - ❑ a. republic.
   - ❑ b. dictatorship.
   - ❑ c. constitutional monarchy.

2. Parliament is made up of the
   - ❑ a. peers and church officials.
   - ❑ b. king or queen and the peers.
   - ❑ c. House of Lords and the House of Commons.

3. The first English kings were
   - ❑ a. barons.
   - ❑ b. warlords.
   - ❑ c. commoners.

4. The Magna Carta stated that
   - ❑ a. the king could not make new taxes without Parliament's consent.
   - ❑ b. people could not be put in jail without a trial.
   - ❑ c. the House of Commons would have the same powers as the House of Lords.

5. The Bill of Rights
   - ❑ a. was signed by King John.
   - ❑ b. was written by Baron Simon de Montfort.
   - ❑ c. gave Parliament more power than the king or queen.

Understanding Ideas

6. It is likely that the barons could force the monarch to share power with them because
   - ❑ a. it would make the commoners happy.
   - ❑ b. kings had always been fair to the barons.
   - ❑ c. the king needed the barons' help to keep the throne.

7. One can infer that throughout England's history
   - ❑ a. many wars were fought for the right to govern.
   - ❑ b. the monarch usually won power struggles with Parliament.
   - ❑ c. power struggles between Parliament and the monarch were peaceful.

8. Compared with the early kings, today's monarch has _____ power.
   - ❑ a. almost no
   - ❑ b. a little less
   - ❑ c. almost the same

9. One can infer that
   - ❑ a. the nobles took power suddenly.
   - ❑ b. Parliament took power over hundreds of years.
   - ❑ c. Parliament and the monarch still share most powers.

10. In this passage, the term *commoners* probably means
    - ❑ a. nobles.
    - ❑ b. people who were not nobles.
    - ❑ c. members of the royal family.

In the Time of Queen Elizabeth I

In 1559 Elizabeth I was crowned Queen of England. She was young, and she faced problems. England was poor. There was the threat of war with Spain. At home, there was unrest. English citizens clashed over religion.

One of Elizabeth's first acts was to make the Church of England the state church. She then worked to keep England out of war. Spain was rich, and it had lands in the New World. Elizabeth sent sailors to pirate Spanish ships. As Spain's ships sailed from the New World, the English robbed them. This brought wealth to England. It put off war with Spain, as Spain had to have money to wage war. Later Spain sent its ships to attack England. The English ships defeated them.

Elizabeth reigned until her death in 1603. She made England rich and strong. Her reign was a time of world discovery. She sent the first English settlers to the New World. The colonies gave Britain greater power in the world. Elizabeth's reign was a time of rebirth of the arts. Literature and art flourished. The era was called the Renaissance. It began in Italy and spread to England. Elizabeth's court was a place where writers, musicians, and scholars worked. William Shakespeare wrote his plays at this time. Elizabeth's reign is called the Golden Age of English history.

1. **Recognizing Words in Context**

   Find the word *clashed* in the passage. One definition below is closest to the meaning of that word. One definition has the opposite or nearly the opposite meaning. The remaining definition has a completely different meaning. Label the definitions C for *closest,* O for *opposite or nearly opposite,* and D for *different.*

   _____ a. agreed

   _____ b. fought

   _____ c. sounded

2. **Distinguishing Fact from Opinion**

   Two of the statements below present *facts,* which can be proved. The other statement is an *opinion,* which expresses someone's thoughts or beliefs. Label the statements F for *fact* and O for *opinion.*

   _____ a. Elizabeth I sent the first English settlers to the New World.

   _____ b. Elizabeth I was England's greatest queen.

   _____ c. William Shakespeare wrote plays during the reign of Elizabeth I.

3. Keeping Events in Order

Number the statements below 1, 2, and 3 to show the order in which the events took place.

_____ a. Elizabeth I sent the first English settlers to the New World.

_____ b. Elizabeth I made the Church of England the state church.

_____ c. Elizabeth I was crowned Queen of England.

4. Making Correct Inferences

Two of the statements below are correct *inferences,* or reasonable guesses. They are based on information in the passage. The other statement is an incorrect, or faulty, inference. Label the statements C for *correct* inference and F for *faulty* inference.

_____ a. The reign of Elizabeth I is known as the Golden Age of English history because it was a time of great achievements.

_____ b. Elizabeth I started the era called the Renaissance.

_____ c. Elizabeth I reigned for more than 40 years and did much to help her country.

5. Understanding Main Ideas

One of the statements below expresses the main idea of the passage. One statement is too general, or too broad. The other explains only part of the passage; it is too narrow. Label the statements M for *main idea*, B for *too broad*, and N for *too narrow*.

_____ a. During the reign of Elizabeth I, world exploration and the arts flourished.

_____ b. Elizabeth I was an English monarch.

_____ c. Elizabeth I of England sent sailors to pirate Spanish ships.

Correct Answers, Part A _____

Correct Answers, Part B _____

Total Correct Answers _____

68

The Inuit: People of the Cold

The Inuit live in the cold climates of the North. They live near the coasts of Greenland, North Siberia, and the Arctic. This area includes parts of Canada and Alaska. *Inuit* means "the people." Today many Inuit live in western-style houses. They wear ready-made clothes and buy food at grocery stores. However, their traditional way of life reflects the climate in which they have lived since early times.

In the Arctic, the treeless ground stays frozen year round. Summers are short, and the sun shines day and night. The temperature may rise to 50 degrees. Winters are long. The sun does not shine for months. Temperatures are subzero. There are snowstorms and strong winds. In the past, the Inuit dressed in layers of fur clothes to keep warm. The women used caribou sinew as thread, and they sewed with bone needles. They made watertight parkas from seal or walrus intestines.

The men hunted for the family's food. Families ate fish, seals, whales, polar bears, hares, foxes, and sea birds. To hunt, the Inuit traveled over the ice and snow on dog sleds. The sleds had whalebone runners. They were pulled by native dogs. Hunters used harpoons of bone or walrus tusk to spear their prey. They might wait for hours by an ice hole for a walrus to come up for air. They also hunted by boat. One boat, a kayak, is a canoe-like craft covered with sealskin. One person sits in the boat, and the skin is laced up around him. Another boat is called a umiak. It is an open boat made for more than one person. Hunters teamed up to hunt walruses or whales.

Families lived in igloos built by the men. The word *igloo* means "house." A winter house was a hut usually made of sod or stone. The frame for the roof was made of whalebone. The roof was covered with sod, moss, or walrus hides. Inside the igloo, the Inuit slept on a platform of furs. Heat and light came from stone lamps that burned animal fat. Fuel was not often used for cooking. Most meat was eaten raw. In the spring, melting snow would collapse the roof. The men would build a new house somewhere else the next winter. Domes built of snow blocks were used as shelter on long trips. In the summer, the people lived in tents made of hides.

Reading Time _____

Recalling Facts

1. *Inuit* means
   - ❑ a. the people.
   - ❑ b. the cold people.
   - ❑ c. the northern people.

2. Winter temperatures in the Arctic are
   - ❑ a. subzero.
   - ❑ b. around freezing.
   - ❑ c. as warm as 50 degrees Fahrenheit.

3. A canoelike craft for one person that is covered with sealskin is a
   - ❑ a. sled.
   - ❑ b. umiak.
   - ❑ c. kayak.

4. The word *igloo* means
   - ❑ a. boat.
   - ❑ b. house.
   - ❑ c. snow block.

5. Most meat was
   - ❑ a. eaten raw.
   - ❑ b. cooked in a large pot.
   - ❑ c. smoked over a stone lamp.

Understanding Ideas

6. Which sentence best tells what the whole passage is about?
   - ❑ a. In the Arctic, summers are short and winters are long.
   - ❑ b. The cold climate in which the Inuit live shaped their traditional way of life.
   - ❑ c. The Inuit live near the coasts of Greenland, North Siberia, and the Arctic.

7. From the passage, one can infer that
   - ❑ a. hunting was difficult and took time.
   - ❑ b. it was easy for the Inuit to find food.
   - ❑ c. most hunting took place near the igloos.

8. It is likely that the Inuit can survive for a long time without
   - ❑ a. animals.
   - ❑ b. each other.
   - ❑ c. sunshine.

9. From the passage, one can infer that Inuit men and women
   - ❑ a. hunted together.
   - ❑ b. lived in separate igloos.
   - ❑ c. did different kinds of work.

10. An early Inuit who wanted to make a tool would be least likely to make it from
    - ❑ a. wood.
    - ❑ b. bone.
    - ❑ c. stone.

15　B　Inuit Art

The Inuit way of life is expressed in their art. For hundreds of years, the Inuit made art from things they had at hand such as ivory. Ivory comes from walrus tusks or whale teeth. They carved the ivory into figures of people and animals. They shaped it into useful things such as knobs and tools. Their carvings had decorative designs. The art of carving on ivory is called scrimshaw. The Inuit also carved antlers, musk ox horn, and stone. They used ivory and bone to make jewelry. They used whalebone or driftwood to carve masks. Some masks were very small, and others were huge.

The Inuit have made dolls for at least 1,000 years. Heads were made of leather or soapstone. Fur was used for hair. Dolls were dressed in clothes of fur and skins. By cutting and sewing dolls, Inuit girls learned skills they would use later to make waterproof clothing. Some dolls were so small they could be carried in a mitten.

When the first Europeans came, the Inuit used carvings for trade. The women made fur clothes to trade.

Today Inuit artists still make carvings, jewelry, dolls, and clothes. Some clothing is made from wool. Their art now includes painting, pottery, and cloth pictures. Inuit art reflects both past and present Inuit life.

1. **Recognizing Words in Context**

Find the word *decorative* in the passage. One definition below is closest to the meaning of that word. One definition has the opposite or nearly the opposite meaning. The remaining definition has a completely different meaning. Label the definitions C for *closest*, O for *opposite or nearly opposite*, and D for *different*.

_____ a. different

_____ b. fancy

_____ c. plain

2. **Distinguishing Fact from Opinion**

Two of the statements below present *facts*, which can be proved. The other statement is an *opinion*, which expresses someone's thoughts or beliefs. Label the statements F for *fact* and O for *opinion*.

_____ a. The Inuit have made dolls for at least 1,000 years.

_____ b. The art of carving on ivory is called scrimshaw.

_____ c. Inuit carvings are far more beautiful than carvings made by other native peoples.

3. Keeping Events in Order

Number the statements below 1, 2, and 3 to show the order in which the events took place.

_____ a. When the first Europeans came, the Inuit used carvings for trade.

_____ b. For hundreds of years, the Inuit made art from what they had at hand.

_____ c. Today Inuit artists still use native materials for carving.

4. Making Correct Inferences

Two of the statements below are correct *inferences,* or reasonable guesses. They are based on information in the passage. The other statement is an incorrect, or faulty, inference. Label the statements C for *correct* inference and F for *faulty* inference.

_____ a. Most Inuit art today is made from wool.

_____ b. The early Inuit made very little art from wood.

_____ c. Early Inuit artists carved designs on tools and other useful objects.

5. Understanding Main Ideas

One of the statements below expresses the main idea of the passage. One statement is too general, or too broad. The other explains only part of the passage; it is too narrow. Label the statements M for *main idea*, B for *too broad*, and N for *too narrow.*

_____ a. For centuries the traditional Inuit way of life has been expressed in their art.

_____ b. Whalebone or driftwood was used to carve masks.

_____ c. The Inuit have created art for hundreds of years.

Correct Answers, Part A _____

Correct Answers, Part B _____

Total Correct Answers _____

The First Voyage of Columbus

Christopher Columbus was an Italian explorer in the fifteenth century. At that time, people did not think of the world the way they do today. Many people thought the world was flat. Exploring new lands took courage. Explorers had to be willing to go into the unknown. Many people believed sea monsters living in the ocean would attack a ship. Some were afraid they would fall off the edge of the earth if they traveled too far.

Columbus thought he could find a way to the Indies by sailing west. This would be a good trade route. Columbus tried to get help from the king of Portugal. The king said no. So Columbus went to King Ferdinand and Queen Isabella of Spain. Spain wanted new land to add to its empire. With a better trade route, Spain would be able to buy things such as spices and silk. Even so, it took Columbus almost seven years to convince the king and queen. Finally they said yes. Columbus could begin his voyage.

He assembled three ships. They were the *Niña,* the *Pinta,* and the *Santa Maria*. He recruited a crew of about 85 men. On August 3, 1492, he sailed west from Palos, Spain. Columbus sailed on the *Santa Maria*. It was the largest of the three ships. On the trip, the ships stopped for supplies in the Canary Islands. Then they continued southwest.

The journey was very hard. The work on the ships was exhausting. At that time, ships used for exploration had to carry enough supplies for very long periods of time. No one knew how long a ship might have to be out in the open sea. Food often spoiled. Water was in short supply.

Because no one could be sure Columbus would find what he was looking for, members of the crew were afraid. After several weeks at sea, they wanted to turn back. Columbus refused. Some say there was talk of mutiny. A number of the men were sick. They couldn't see land. Columbus asked the crew to wait three more days. The next day they saw a flock of birds. This meant land must be close by. Soon they saw dolphins and a tree branch. On October 12, 1492, the ships landed on an island in the Bahamas. Columbus, however, thought he had found an island off the coast of Asia. Columbus named the island San Salvador.

Reading Time _____

Recalling Facts

1. The work on Columbus's ships was
   - ❏ a. well paid.
   - ❏ b. very difficult.
   - ❏ c. decent and pleasant.

2. Columbus received support for his journey from
   - ❏ a. Spain.
   - ❏ b. Portugal.
   - ❏ c. the West Indies.

3. Columbus's crew knew land was nearby because they saw
   - ❏ a. a lighthouse.
   - ❏ b. another ship.
   - ❏ c. a flock of birds.

4. At the time of Columbus, many people thought the earth was
   - ❏ a. flat.
   - ❏ b. round.
   - ❏ c. square.

5. The ship on which Columbus sailed from Spain was the
   - ❏ a. *Pinta.*
   - ❏ b. *Niña.*
   - ❏ c. *Santa Maria.*

Understanding Ideas

6. Which of the following sentences best tells what the whole passage is about?
   - ❏ a. Columbus began his journey with three ships.
   - ❏ b. Travel across the ocean in the fifteenth century was dangerous.
   - ❏ c. With help from the King and Queen of Spain, Columbus took three ships across the ocean.

7. It is probable that the King and Queen of Spain supported Columbus because they
   - ❏ a. were sea explorers themselves.
   - ❏ b. thought Columbus could bring them riches.
   - ❏ c. wanted to find out if the world was flat.

8. A character trait that Columbus likely had is
   - ❏ a. greed.
   - ❏ b. laziness.
   - ❏ c. bravery.

9. One can conclude from the passage that Spain wanted new lands to
   - ❏ a. increase its wealth and power.
   - ❏ b. provide more food for its people.
   - ❏ c. understand more about the world's geography.

10. Compared with ship travel in the fifteenth century, ship travel today is
    - ❏ a. less efficient.
    - ❏ b. more dangerous.
    - ❏ c. safer and more reliable.

Christopher Columbus sailed to the New World with three ships. These ships were the *Niña*, the *Pinta*, and the *Santa Maria*. Each ship was slightly different. Life on all three ships was hard. Food was scarce and frequently spoiled.

The *Niña* was a caravel. Caravels were small sailing ships. They were designed to travel in the wind on the open ocean. They could not carry much cargo. Explorers often used caravels. The *Niña* was the smallest and fastest of the three ships. The *Niña* was Columbus's favorite ship. He returned to Spain aboard her. He also used her for many later trips.

The *Pinta* was a caravel too. The *Pinta* was slightly larger and slower than the *Niña*. The *Pinta* returned to Spain with Columbus's crew. But no one is sure what happened to the *Pinta* after that. Some say that she made a few trips to the Caribbean before sinking in a storm.

The *Santa Maria* was the fleet's flagship. It was a *nao*, which was made to carry cargo. This kind of ship was slow. It was not meant for explorers. The *Santa Maria* was the largest ship, so Columbus chose to captain that ship on his first journey. The ship ran aground in the New World and sank.

1. **Recognizing Words in Context**

   Find the word *scarce* in the passage. One definition below is closest to the meaning of that word. One definition has the opposite or nearly the opposite meaning. The remaining definition has a completely different meaning. Label the definitions C for *closest*, O for *opposite or nearly opposite*, and D for *different*.

   _____ a. plentiful

   _____ b. perfect

   _____ c. limited

2. **Distinguishing Fact from Opinion**

   Two of the statements below present *facts*, which can be proved. The other statement is an *opinion*, which expresses someone's thoughts or beliefs. Label the statements F for *fact* and O for *opinion*.

   _____ a. The *Santa Maria* was the best looking ship in Columbus's fleet.

   _____ b. The *Santa Maria* was designed to carry cargo.

   _____ c. The *Niña* was a smaller ship than the *Pinta*.

3. Keeping Events in Order

Number the statements below 1, 2, and 3 to show the order in which the events took place.

_____ a. The *Pinta* returned to Spain with Columbus's crew.

_____ b. Columbus assembled a fleet to sail to the New World.

_____ c. The *Santa Maria* ran aground.

4. Making Correct Inferences

Two of the statements below are correct *inferences,* or reasonable guesses. They are based on information in the passage. The other statement is an incorrect, or faulty, inference. Label the statements C for *correct* inference and F for *faulty* inference.

_____ a. The *Santa Maria* was a larger ship because it was designed to carry cargo.

_____ b. Explorers used caravels because they were swift.

_____ c. The *Santa Maria* was not a good ship.

5. Understanding Main Ideas

One of the statements below expresses the main idea of the passage. One statement is too general, or too broad. The other explains only part of the passage; it is too narrow. Label the statements M for *main idea,* B for *too broad,* and N for *too narrow.*

_____ a. Many explorers in the fifteenth century, such as Columbus, used ships to find new lands.

_____ b. The *Niña* was Columbus's favorite ship, and he used her for many trips after his first voyage to the New World.

_____ c. Columbus's three ships— the *Niña,* the *Pinta,* and the *Santa Maria*—offered different advantages and experienced different fates.

Correct Answers, Part A _____

Correct Answers, Part B _____

Total Correct Answers _____

History is a record of the people and events of the past. The study of history shows how the past has shaped today's world. History is a basic part of everyone's schooling. Teachers in this field have a firm grasp of social studies. They have an in-depth knowledge of the human past. They usually like to study maps and read stories about people's lives.

To be a history teacher, a person must have training and skills. Someone who wants to teach must have a college degree. A training program is useful as well. Teachers must be able to communicate well. They must know how to present information to their students. Teachers must know how to manage a classroom. They need to enjoy working with young people.

Students who want to be history teachers can begin to gain the skills they need in high school. They can take social studies courses. They can tutor classmates. They can work with young children. Learning about social studies and knowing how to work with others can prepare students for their college studies.

People who want to teach history must earn college degrees in the field. They complete courses in U.S. and world history. They learn about diverse peoples and ways of life. They may study foreign languages as well.

While in college, some students join teacher-training programs. They take classes in teaching methods. Such courses help new teachers learn to work with students. In their last year of college, students in teaching programs act as student teachers. They work in junior high or high school classrooms. Skilled history teachers observe them and help them.

More and more, those who wish to be teachers work toward advanced degrees after college. Many earn master's degrees. Master's programs often take two years. These degrees open the doors to better jobs.

Once trained, a teacher must obtain a license or a certificate. States usually require teachers to pass one or more exams before they get their licenses.

A new teacher can find a job in many ways. Schools often recruit teachers. They post job ads at teacher-training schools. They also use job sites on the World Wide Web. Once a teacher applies for a job, the school asks for an interview. If this meeting goes well, the school may make a job offer. In this way, a history teacher secures a job in the classroom.

Reading Time _____

Recalling Facts

1. History is
   - ❑ a. a story from the past.
   - ❑ b. the study of all forms of life.
   - ❑ c. a record of people and events of the past.

2. To teach history, a person must
   - ❑ a. earn a degree in history.
   - ❑ b. take one history course in college.
   - ❑ c. work under the guidance of a skilled teacher for three years.

3. Students can first begin to acquire the skills they need to be a teacher
   - ❑ a. when they become adults.
   - ❑ b. by tutoring classmates in high school.
   - ❑ c. by working with a skilled teacher when they are in college.

4. Students take classes to become trained teachers
   - ❑ a. in history programs.
   - ❑ b. in teacher-training programs.
   - ❑ c. in high school.

5. After college, a person who wants to become a teacher must
   - ❑ a. get a license.
   - ❑ b. learn a foreign language.
   - ❑ c. go back to school for a master's degree.

Understanding Ideas

6. A topic most likely studied in history is
   - ❑ a. the cause of an earthquake.
   - ❑ b. the lives of early coal miners.
   - ❑ c. the future of the space program.

7. One can conclude from the passage that someone becomes a teacher after completing
   - ❑ a. high school.
   - ❑ b. three teaching courses.
   - ❑ c. college and teacher training.

8. A task likely to prepare high school students to teach is
   - ❑ a. watching the news.
   - ❑ b. reading children's books.
   - ❑ c. working with children in an after-school program.

9. One can conclude from the passage that a master's degree is _____ for teachers.
   - ❑ a. useful
   - ❑ b. required
   - ❑ c. not at all useful

10. One can conclude from the passage that a new teacher obtains a job by
    - ❑ a. working as a substitute teacher.
    - ❑ b. applying and interviewing for teaching jobs.
    - ❑ c. waiting for the state to offer jobs to new teachers.

Ivan borrowed a library book from Nick. He finished reading it. Then he left the book in the basket on Nick's bike without telling Nick. The next day Nick asked Ivan to return the book. Ivan told Nick that he had returned the book. But the book was gone. Nick was angry. He felt that Ivan should help him pay for the library book. Ivan did not agree.

Ms. Chen noticed Nick's anger. She took him aside to talk about the problem. Then she asked Nick and Ivan to discuss their conflict in social studies class. They agreed.

Ms. Chen explained the day's lesson to the class. They were going to learn about resolving conflicts. Without taking sides, the class would help the two students work out their differences. Ms. Chen asked Nick and Ivan to tell their stories. The class then asked questions. Nick and Ivan worked together to define their problem. Ms. Chen asked them to identify solutions. The class added ideas to the list of solutions. Soon, Nick and Ivan agreed to a resolution. They would share the cost of the lost book. They signed an agreement and shook hands. Nick did not feel angry anymore. He felt that, with the help of the class, he and Ivan had reached an equitable solution.

1. **Recognizing Words in Context**

   Find the word *equitable* in the passage. One definition below is closest to the meaning of that word. One definition has the opposite or nearly the opposite meaning. The remaining definition has a completely different meaning. Label the definitions C for *closest*, O for *opposite or nearly opposite*, and D for *different*.

   _____ a. fair

   _____ b. quick

   _____ c. unjust

2. **Distinguishing Fact from Opinion**

   Two of the statements below present *facts*, which can be proved. The other statement is an *opinion*, which expresses someone's thoughts or beliefs. Label the statements F for *fact* and O for *opinion*.

   _____ a. Nick and Ivan agreed to a solution.

   _____ b. Ivan was to blame for the lost book.

   _____ c. Ms. Chen gave a social studies lesson on conflict resolution.

3. **Keeping Events in Order**

   Number the statements below 1, 2, and 3 to show the order in which the events took place.

   _____ a. Nick and Ivan tell their stories.

   _____ b. With the help of the class, Nick and Ivan define the conflict.

   _____ c. Nick and Ivan work together to find a solution to their problem.

4. **Making Correct Inferences**

   Two of the statements below are correct *inferences*, or reasonable guesses. They are based on information in the passage. The other statement is an incorrect, or faulty, inference. Label the statements C for *correct* inference and F for *faulty* inference.

   _____ a. The class helped Nick and Ivan work out their problem.

   _____ b. Ms. Chen was the one who solved Nick and Ivan's problem.

   _____ c. Defining the problem and proposing solutions are key steps in resolving conflicts.

5. **Understanding Main Ideas**

   One of the statements below expresses the main idea of the passage. One statement is too general, or too broad. The other explains only part of the passage; it is too narrow. Label the statements M for *main idea*, B for *too broad*, and N for *too narrow*.

   _____ a. Nick and Ivan use conflict resolution skills to solve a problem.

   _____ b. Resolving conflict is an important skill for today's youth.

   _____ c. With the help of the class, Nick and Ivan define their problem.

Correct Answers, Part A _____

Correct Answers, Part B _____

Total Correct Answers _____

Imagine a relay race. An athlete holding a baton runs a certain distance. Then he passes it to the next runner. That person runs on farther and then passes the baton to a third runner. Now imagine that the runners are not passing a baton. They are passing silk, gold, spices, fruit, and glass. Imagine that the race does not move forward in just one direction. Instead, each runner goes back and forth along a path, trading goods at each end of his route. Now suppose that the runners are merchants leading caravans of camels. They earn their living by traveling the ancient Silk Road.

The Silk Road was a complex trading network. It passed through thousands of cities and towns. It stretched from eastern China, across Central Asia and the Middle East, to the Mediterranean Sea. It was used from about 200 B.C. to about A.D. 1300, when sea travel offered new routes. It was sometimes called the world's longest highway. However, the Silk Road was a series of routes, not one smooth path. The routes crossed mountains and skirted deserts. They passed through what are now 18 countries. The Silk Road had many dangers. These dangers ranged from scorching sun and deep snow to bandits and battles. Only expert traders could survive.

The Silk Road got its name from its most prized product. Silk could be used like money to pay taxes or buy goods. But the traders carried more than just silk. Gold, silver, and glass from Europe were much sought after in the Middle East and Asia. Horses traded from the steppe region changed farming and military practices in China and other regions. Indian merchants traded salt, spices, and precious gems. Chinese merchants traded porcelain and medicine. They also traded paper, which quickly replaced parchment in the West. Apples traveled from central Asia to Rome. The Chinese had learned to graft different trees together to make new kinds of fruit. They passed this science on to others, including the Romans. The Romans used grafting to domesticate the apple. Trading along the Silk Road led to widespread global commerce 2,000 years before the World Wide Web.

The people along the Silk Road did not share just goods. They also shared their beliefs. Monks, priests, and others taught people along the Silk Road about their religions. The Silk Road created pathways for learning, diplomacy, and religion.

Reading Time _____

Recalling Facts

1. The Silk Road was a
   - ❑ a. smooth paved road.
   - ❑ b. uneven country road.
   - ❑ c. series of dangerous routes.

2. The Silk Road's name came from
   - ❑ a. its most valuable product.
   - ❑ b. the smoothness of the route.
   - ❑ c. the hundreds of silk weavers along the route.

3. The Silk Road extended from
   - ❑ a. China to eastern India.
   - ❑ b. eastern China to England.
   - ❑ c. eastern China to the Mediterranean Sea.

4. Each caravan trader traveled
   - ❑ a. from one end of the Silk Road to the other.
   - ❑ b. from city to city along the Silk Road.
   - ❑ c. back and forth along a section of the Silk Road.

5. Trade along the Silk Road was most active from
   - ❑ a. 100 B.C. to A.D. 1600.
   - ❑ b. 200 B.C. to A.D. 1300.
   - ❑ c. 500 B.C. to A.D. 1000.

Understanding Ideas

6. It is probable that caravan traders needed to know
   - ❑ a. more than one language.
   - ❑ b. how to make the products they traded.
   - ❑ c. the entire trade route from China to the Mediterranean.

7. Goods along the Silk Road were traded
   - ❑ a. from east to west.
   - ❑ b. from west to east.
   - ❑ c. in every direction on the compass.

8. Trade along the Silk Road can be compared with exchanges
   - ❑ a. at a shopping mall.
   - ❑ b. at a local supermarket.
   - ❑ c. on the World Wide Web.

9. The Silk Road declined because
   - ❑ a. the caravan leaders wanted to settle down.
   - ❑ b. people didn't need any more foreign goods.
   - ❑ c. sea travel became easier than crossing mountains and deserts.

10. New technologies, such as making paper and grafting trees, could travel along the Silk Road because people
    - ❑ a. sent spies to steal trade secrets.
    - ❑ b. learned from one another.
    - ❑ c. read about the new technologies in the newspaper.

18 B   What Is Silk and How Is It Made?

Legend has it that a Chinese empress found the secrets of silk 5,000 years ago. The empress was walking by a mulberry tree. All at once, a silkworm's cocoon fell into her tea and unwound. For thousands of years, China safeguarded the secrets of silk. It was the only place in the world to find this warm, lightweight, lavish fabric. After trading began along the Silk Road, the secret spread to other countries.

Silk comes from the cocoon of the silkworm moth. A caterpillar hatches from the moth's egg. It spends nearly a month eating mulberry leaves. It will eat nothing else. Then it spins a cocoon. This takes about three days. To make the cocoon, the silkworm secretes, or gives off, two substances from its head. The first is a liquid protein. This hardens in the air into silk fiber. The second is a sticky jelly. The jelly holds the fiber in place. The caterpillar winds the fiber around itself into a tight case.

The cocoon is dropped into hot water so the jelly will melt. When the fiber loosens, it can be unwound. Each cocoon is made of one fiber more than a mile long. Five to ten fibers must be spun together to make a thread of silk. Silk thread can be used for weaving, knitting, or sewing.

1. **Recognizing Words in Context**

Find the word *safeguarded* in the passage. One definition below is closest to the meaning of that word. One definition has the opposite or nearly the opposite meaning. The remaining definition has a completely different meaning. Label the definitions C for *closest*, O for *opposite or nearly opposite*, and D for *different*.

_____ a. remembered

_____ b. protected

_____ c. attacked

2. **Distinguishing Fact from Opinion**

Two of the statements below present *facts*, which can be proved. The other statement is an *opinion*, which expresses someone's thoughts or beliefs. Label the statements F for *fact* and O for *opinion*.

_____ a. Silk comes from the cocoon of the silkworm.

_____ b. Silk is warm and lightweight.

_____ c. Silk is the best fabric one can buy.

3. Keeping Events in Order

Number the statements below 1, 2, and 3 to show the order in which the events took place.

_____ a. The silkworm secretes liquid protein and jelly.

_____ b. The silkworm eats mulberry leaves for almost a month.

_____ c. The silkworm's cocoon is dropped into hot water to melt the jelly.

4. Making Correct Inferences

Two of the statements below are correct *inferences,* or reasonable guesses. They are based on information in the passage. The other statement is an incorrect, or faulty, inference. Label the statements C for *correct* inference and F for *faulty* inference.

_____ a. Because China guarded the secrets of silk-making, it could charge higher prices for silk goods.

_____ b. The more trade increased along the Silk Road, the harder it was to protect the secrets of silk-making.

_____ c. The silk-making industry in China ended when others found out how to make silk.

5. Understanding Main Ideas

One of the statements below expresses the main idea of the passage. One statement is too general, or too broad. The other explains only part of the passage; it is too narrow. Label the statements M for *main idea,* B for *too broad,* and N for *too narrow.*

_____ a. Silk, a valuable product originated in China, is made by the silkworm and then processed by people.

_____ b. Once a silkworm caterpillar hatches from its egg, it spends nearly a month eating mulberry leaves.

_____ c. Silk and other fine fabrics are made in many places around the world.

Correct Answers, Part A _____

Correct Answers, Part B _____

Total Correct Answers _____

Symbols help unite a group or a country. Three important symbols of the United States are the Liberty Bell, the bald eagle, and the Statue of Liberty.

The Liberty Bell is a symbol of freedom. The first bell was cast in London in 1752. It had been ordered by the Pennsylvania Assembly for its State House. The bell was hung in Philadelphia in 1753. The first time it was rung to test its sound, it cracked. Two workers cast a new bell. They used the metal from the British bell. This bell rang only for special events. It rang on July 8, 1776, at the first public reading of the Declaration of Independence. The last time the bell rang was in 1846, when it rang for George Washington's birthday. The bell cracked, creating the zigzag fracture it still has today. The bell is on display in Philadelphia.

The bald eagle is our national emblem. It was chosen in 1782. The eagle lives on top of a mountain. It has unlimited freedom in its flight. This made it a good choice for a new nation focused on freedom and liberty. The bald eagle has a long life. It can live for more than 30 years in the wild. This made it a great symbol for the long life the founders hoped America would enjoy. The eagle appears on the Great Seal of the United States and on other patriotic items, such as state flags.

The Statue of Liberty is a much newer symbol of the nation. The statue is located in New York. It was a gift from the people of France. They raised the money for the statue. They hoped to have it ready by 1876. They wanted to honor the United States on its 100th birthday. But they did not have enough money to complete it until 1886. The designer broke the statue down into 350 pieces to ship it to New York by boat. Once it arrived, crews took four months to rebuild it. The people of the United States helped create this symbol too. They raised the money to build the pedestal. The statue measures 305 feet from the ground to the tip of the torch. There are seven rays in the statue's crown. These rays stand for the seven seas and the seven continents. The Statue of Liberty stands as a symbol of freedom to people around the world.

Reading Time _____

Recalling Facts

1. The first Liberty Bell was cast in
   - ❑ a. London.
   - ❑ b. New York.
   - ❑ c. Philadelphia.

2. The last time the Liberty Bell rang was at a celebration for
   - ❑ a. Washington's birthday.
   - ❑ b. the end of the Civil War.
   - ❑ c. the beginning of the Revolutionary War.

3. One reason the bald eagle was chosen as a national symbol is because of its
   - ❑ a. long life.
   - ❑ b. sharp talons.
   - ❑ c. white feathers.

4. The people of the United States helped contribute to the Statue of Liberty by paying for the
   - ❑ a. designer.
   - ❑ b. pedestal.
   - ❑ c. shipping charges.

5. The seven rays in the Statue of Liberty's crown stand for the seven
   - ❑ a. seas and seven continents.
   - ❑ b. wars fought for freedom.
   - ❑ c. artists who worked on the statue.

Understanding Ideas

6. One can conclude from the passage that the United States wants its symbols to
   - ❑ a. be hard to recognize.
   - ❑ b. be important only to Americans.
   - ❑ c. represent freedom to the whole world.

7. In contrast to the Liberty Bell and the Statue of Liberty, the bald eagle is not
   - ❑ a. located at a specific site.
   - ❑ b. accepted by most Americans.
   - ❑ c. well known outside of the United States.

8. One can conclude from the passage that France
   - ❑ a. also supported the idea of freedom.
   - ❑ b. did not think that the United States was free.
   - ❑ c. wanted to become part of the United States.

9. One can conclude from the passage that
   - ❑ a. every country has the same symbols.
   - ❑ b. symbols are important to many people.
   - ❑ c. a country with symbols always supports freedom.

10. It is likely that the nation's founders thought the United States would
    - ❑ a. remain free.
    - ❑ b. be reclaimed by Britain.
    - ❑ c. exist for only a short time.

Most people think Betsy Ross sewed the first U.S. flag. But recently people have begun to question this idea. It is known that she was one of the people who sewed an early flag. But no one is sure who sewed the very first flag. However, of those first people to sew the flag, Ross is the best known.

Betsy Ross worked as an upholsterer. In those days, it was common for an upholsterer to do many kinds of sewing. This included sewing flags. George Washington and Betsy Ross knew each other. They attended the same church. Ross had sewn many items for Washington in the past. In 1776 Washington asked her to sew a flag.

Her flag is known as the Betsy Ross flag. It has 13 stripes, seven red and six white. The stripes stand for the 13 colonies. The flag has 13 stars arranged in a circle. The stars represent a constellation in the night sky. This is a group of stars in the night sky. This design shows equality. No colony had more power than another. No one knows what happened to the first flag. Very few flags survive from that time.

The flag design changed as more states joined the nation. Now the flag has 50 stars, one for each state.

1. **Recognizing Words in Context**

   Find the word *equality* in the passage. One definition below is closest to the meaning of that word. One definition has the opposite or nearly the opposite meaning. The remaining definition has a completely different meaning. Label the definitions C for *closest*, O for *opposite or nearly opposite*, and D for *different*.

   _____ a. improvement

   _____ b. injustice

   _____ c. sameness

2. **Distinguishing Fact from Opinion**

   Two of the statements below present *facts*, which can be proved. The other statement is an *opinion*, which expresses someone's thoughts or beliefs. Label the statements F for *fact* and O for *opinion*.

   _____ a. Betsy Ross was the best upholsterer.

   _____ b. Betsy Ross sewed one of the first U.S. flags.

   _____ c. The first U.S. flag had 13 stars.

3. Keeping Events in Order

Number the statements below 1, 2, and 3 to show the order in which the events took place.

_____ a. George Washington asked Betsy Ross to sew a flag.

_____ b. The flag design changed.

_____ c. Betsy Ross sewed items for George Washington.

4. Making Correct Inferences

Two of the statements below are correct *inferences,* or reasonable guesses. They are based on information in the passage. The other statement is an incorrect, or faulty, inference. Label the statements C for *correct* inference and F for *faulty* inference.

_____ a. Betsy Ross was the only one to sew a U.S. flag with 13 stars.

_____ b. Many people have helped create the flag design of today.

_____ c. George Washington thought Betsy Ross would do a good job on the flag.

5. Understanding Main Ideas

One of the statements below expresses the main idea of the passage. One statement is too general, or too broad. The other explains only part of the passage; it is too narrow. Label the statements M for *main idea,* B for *too broad,* and N for *too narrow.*

_____ a. The first U.S. flag had 13 stars.

_____ b. Betsy Ross was one of the first people to sew a U.S. flag.

_____ c. The U.S. flag is an important symbol throughout the world.

Correct Answers, Part A _____

Correct Answers, Part B _____

Total Correct Answers _____

Henry Ford and the First Assembly Line

In 1913 Henry Ford built the first conveyor-belt assembly line. It was in his Model T car factory. He started with an assembly line for just one part of the car. It had taken 20 minutes to make that one part. With the assembly line, it took only 5 minutes. So he put in more assembly lines. They cut the time needed to make a car from 17 hours to just 93 minutes.

Ford's assembly line combined three key ideas. The first idea was breaking a big job into smaller tasks. This had been done in the textile industry. One person used to do all the tasks needed to turn cotton into cloth. However, in the 1700s, factories divided the work into smaller tasks. One group would just spin cotton. Another group would thread the loom. By breaking the work into smaller tasks, workers specialized in one part of making cloth.

The second idea made sure that work flowed at a smooth pace. All the things needed to perform a task were ready at the right time. No time was wasted. In the 1800s, meatpackers in Chicago had found a way to make work flow evenly. They built a machine that could move meat from worker to worker at an even pace. Each worker had a station and a task. The machine brought meat to the station just long enough for the worker to do the task. The machine kept the meat moving from station to station.

The third idea was to build machines with standardized parts. In the past, workers made each part by hand. No two parts were exactly alike. For instance, the parts used to make a gun were very complex. It took a long time to make each part and then to fit the parts together to make a gun. In 1797 Eli Whitney found a way to make gun parts by machine. The machine could make parts quickly, and the parts were standardized.

Henry Ford was the first to put all three of these ideas together. In his Model T plant, work was broken into small tasks. Each worker had a station and a task. The conveyor belt moved parts from station to station, stopping long enough for the workers to complete their tasks. The car parts were standardized so parts fit together easily. Ford produced Model Ts quicker and cheaper, so many ordinary people were able to buy them.

Reading Time _____

Recalling Facts

1. The first modern conveyor-belt assembly line was in a
   - ❏ a. car factory.
   - ❏ b. textile factory.
   - ❏ c. computer factory.

2. Ford's assembly line helped cut the time to make a car from 17 hours to
   - ❏ a. 9 hours.
   - ❏ b. 12 hours.
   - ❏ c. 93 minutes.

3. Eli Whitney found a way to make guns faster with a
   - ❏ a. conveyor-belt assembly line.
   - ❏ b. machine that quickly made standardized parts.
   - ❏ c. moving machine that brought gun parts from one worker's station to another.

4. Textile factories changed the way cloth was made by
   - ❏ a. insisting that work be done by hand.
   - ❏ b. dividing the work into smaller tasks.
   - ❏ c. using a machine that made work flow at an even pace.

5. Meatpackers found a way to work better with a machine that
   - ❏ a. sharpened tools faster.
   - ❏ b. cut standardized parts.
   - ❏ c. made work flow at a smooth pace.

Understanding Ideas

6. Henry Ford came up with his assembly line by
   - ❏ a. watching carmakers work.
   - ❏ b. building on timesaving ideas already in use.
   - ❏ c. buying a patented process.

7. Ford installed assembly lines in his car factory because he wanted to
   - ❏ a. hire more workers.
   - ❏ b. try something new.
   - ❏ c. make cars more quickly and cheaply.

8. Breaking work into smaller tasks helps work go faster because workers
   - ❏ a. need fewer breaks.
   - ❏ b. have more variety in their days.
   - ❏ c. can concentrate on doing one job well.

9. Work that flows at a smooth pace
   - ❏ a. cuts down on wasted time.
   - ❏ b. lets workers do many tasks at once.
   - ❏ c. leads to fewer assembly line breakdowns.

10. Using standardized parts can help make work flow smoothly and quickly because such parts are
   - ❏ a. made by a machine.
   - ❏ b. unique and specialized.
   - ❏ c. exactly alike and always fit together the same way.

The Impact of Mass Production

The first cars were built in the 1890s. These cars were made by hand, piece by piece. The car makers—or the buyers—could ask for any details they wanted. But the cars cost a lot and took a long time to make. Henry Ford wanted to make cars people could afford. He used standardized parts and a conveyor-belt assembly line to make cars quickly. His cars cost less to make. Millions of people could afford them. By 1927 he had sold 15 million Model T cars.

The Model T did not have as many options as cars have today. In fact, it did not have any options at all. Each Model T was just like all the others. All the cars were black. They were all the same size. They all had the same parts. Using the same parts kept the assembly line moving quickly and smoothly. This method of making the same thing over and over, quickly and cheaply, is called mass production.

Other companies started to use this process. Soon many companies were making goods quickly that people could afford. The process has improved. Now companies can customize their goods with different styles and features. Cars, furniture, dishwashers, computers, and many other products are made today on assembly lines.

1. **Recognizing Words in Context**

   Find the word *customize* in the passage. One definition below is closest to the meaning of that word. One definition has the opposite or nearly the opposite meaning. The remaining definition has a completely different meaning. Label the definitions C for *closest*, O for *opposite or nearly opposite*, and D for *different*.

   _____ a. standardize

   _____ b. specialize

   _____ c. reduce

2. **Distinguishing Fact from Opinion**

   Two of the statements below present *facts*, which can be proved. The other statement is an *opinion*, which expresses someone's thoughts or beliefs. Label the statements F for *fact* and O for *opinion*.

   _____ a. In its time, the Model T was affordable for many people.

   _____ b. In its time, the Model T was the best car available.

   _____ c. All Model T cars were made exactly alike.

3. Keeping Events in Order

Label the statements below 1, 2, and 3 to show the order in which the events happened.

_____ a. Cars made on an assembly line could be customized.

_____ b. Cars were made using an assembly line and standardized parts.

_____ c. Cars were made by hand, piece by piece.

4. Making Correct Inferences

Two of the statements below are correct *inferences,* or reasonable guesses. They are based on information in the passage. The other statement is an incorrect, or faulty, inference. Label the statements C for *correct* inference and F for *faulty* inference.

_____ a. Mass production made products that more people could afford.

_____ b. Mass production improved working conditions in factories.

_____ c. Mass production lowered the cost of making many products.

5. Understanding Main Ideas

One of the statements below expresses the main idea of the passage. One statement is too general, or too broad. The other explains only part of the passage; it is too narrow. Label the statements M for *main idea,* B for *too broad,* and N for *too narrow.*

_____ a. Assembly lines changed the way cars and other products are made.

_____ b. Assembly lines used standardized parts.

_____ c. Assembly lines are used in businesses worldwide.

Correct Answers, Part A _____

Correct Answers, Part B _____

Total Correct Answers _____

The Spanish-American War

The Spanish-American War was a short war. It was fought between the United States and Spain. The war took place in 1898. It lasted only four months. The war was fought on two fronts. Some of the fighting took place in Cuba. Cuba is a country in the Caribbean Sea. Some of the fighting took place in the Philippines. These islands are in the Pacific Ocean.

The Spanish Empire was once very powerful. Since 1492 Spain had been sending explorers around the world. Cuba and the Philippines both belonged to Spain. Spain treated both countries harshly. The people of both countries wanted freedom from Spain's control. People in the United States sympathized with them. But the United States was not ready to go to war with Spain.

Two key events brought the United States and Spain to war. The first was a letter published in the *New York Journal.* This letter was stolen from the Spanish minister in Washington. The letter said bad things about President McKinley. It made people think that Spain was making fun of the United States. A few months later the *U.S.S. Maine,* an American battleship, blew up in a Cuban harbor. Two hundred sixty men died. Many people thought Spain had bombed the ship. However, that was not proved. In March 1898, Senator Redfield Proctor spoke to the Senate about Spain's cruel treatment of the Cuban people. McKinley told Spain to leave Cuba. Five days later the United States declared war on Spain.

Before these events, the United States had wanted to buy Cuba. Cuba had a large sugar cane industry. The United States thought this was very valuable. The United States had invested a great deal of money in Cuba. Spain's harsh treatment of Cuba had harmed U.S. business interests.

The war was the subject of much debate in the United States. Many people felt the United States was being too aggressive. They felt the United States should not try to take new lands. Others thought the country had a duty to spread its way of life throughout the world. This way of thinking is called *manifest destiny.*

The Spanish-American War increased U.S. land holdings. The Treaty of Paris, signed in France in 1898, ended the war. Cuba gained its independence from Spain. The United States now owned Guam, Puerto Rico, and the Philippine Islands. This victory established the United States as a world power.

Reading Time _____

Recalling Facts

1. The Spanish-American War was fought in the Pacific Ocean and the
   - ❏ a. Arctic Ocean.
   - ❏ b. Caribbean Sea.
   - ❏ c. Atlantic Ocean.

2. Cuba once belonged to
   - ❏ a. Spain.
   - ❏ b. the Philippines.
   - ❏ c. the United States.

3. The *U.S.S. Maine* was
   - ❏ a. a U.S. fighter plane.
   - ❏ b. a U.S. battleship.
   - ❏ c. a naval base in southern Florida.

4. The Spanish-American War lasted four
   - ❏ a. years.
   - ❏ b. weeks.
   - ❏ c. months.

5. After the end of the Spanish-American War, the United States owned Guam, the Philippines, and
   - ❏ a. Cuba.
   - ❏ b. Mexico.
   - ❏ c. Puerto Rico.

Understanding Ideas

6. The people of the United States
   - ❏ a. were eager to enter into a war with Spain.
   - ❏ b. were unconcerned with Spain's treatment of the people in Cuba and the Philippines.
   - ❏ c. wanted to enter the war because they felt the United States had been attacked by Spain.

7. As a result of the Spanish-American War, it is likely that the United States
   - ❏ a. weakened its economic power.
   - ❏ b. strengthened its economic power.
   - ❏ c. maintained its economic power.

8. What is the whole passage about?
   - ❏ a. The Spanish-American War was a very short war.
   - ❏ b. The Spanish-American War was important to U.S. expansion and economic development.
   - ❏ c. The Spanish-American War was just one of many wars that was fought over the centuries.

9. A key factor for U.S. involvement in the war was the
   - ❏ a. struggling U.S. farm industry.
   - ❏ b. U.S. investments in Cuba.
   - ❏ c. U.S. agreement with Spain's policies.

10. If Spain had won the Spanish-American War, it is possible that
    - ❏ a. Cuba would have become a U.S. territory.
    - ❏ b. Cuba would have achieved its independence.
    - ❏ c. the United States never would have owned the Philippines, Guam, and Puerto Rico.

Puerto Rico Becomes a United States Territory

Puerto Rico once belonged to Spain. But Puerto Rico has had a troubled history. It has long sought freedom. In 1897 Spain gave Puerto Rico some freedom. But this freedom did not last long.

In 1898 the United States and Spain fought each other in the Spanish-American War. The war lasted four months. Spain surrendered. The United States gained control of Puerto Rico. This meant the country belonged to the United States. Both the United States and Spain signed the Treaty of Paris in France. The treaty made the exchange official.

The United States kept Puerto Rico under military rule until 1900. In 1917 the United States gave the Puerto Rican people U.S. citizenship. In 1952 Puerto Ricans gained the right to elect their own officials. However, Puerto Rico still does not have a representative in the U.S. Congress. Its people cannot vote for the U.S. president. They do not pay federal income taxes.

Puerto Rico's standard of living has improved. Most people can read. Roads are in good shape. People are healthier. The United States has also benefited from the alliance. Puerto Rico is a good naval base for the United States.

People still discuss Puerto Rico's future. Should it become a state? Should it claim independence? Or should it remain a U.S. territory?

1. Recognizing Words in Context

Find the word *surrendered* in the passage. One definition below is closest to the meaning of that word. One definition has the opposite or nearly the opposite meaning. The remaining definition has a completely different meaning. Label the definitions C for *closest*, O for *opposite or nearly opposite*, and D for *different*.

_____ a. practiced

_____ b. fought back

_____ c. quit

2. Distinguishing Fact from Opinion

Two of the statements below present *facts*, which can be proved. The other statement is an *opinion*, which expresses someone's thoughts or beliefs. Label the statements F for *fact* and O for *opinion*.

_____ a. Puerto Rico is a U.S. naval base.

_____ b. Puerto Ricans are U.S. citizens.

_____ c. Puerto Rico would be better off as a state than a U.S. territory.

3. Keeping Events in Order

Number the statements below 1, 2, and 3 to show the order in which the events took place.

_____ a. Puerto Ricans were granted U.S. citizenship.

_____ b. Puerto Rico was a Spanish colony.

_____ c. Puerto Rico became a U.S. territory.

4. Making Correct Inferences

Two of the statements below are correct *inferences*, or reasonable guesses. They are based on information in the passage. The other statement is an incorrect, or faulty, inference. Label the statements C for *correct* inference and F for *faulty* inference.

_____ a. If Spain had won the Spanish-American War, Puerto Rico might still be a Spanish colony.

_____ b. Puerto Ricans enjoy some, but not all, rights of U.S. citizenship.

_____ c. All Puerto Ricans want independence from the United States.

5. Understanding Main Ideas

One of the statements below expresses the main idea of the passage. One statement is too general, or too broad. The other explains only part of the passage; it is too narrow. Label the statements M for *main idea,* B for *too broad,* and N for *too narrow.*

_____ a. Puerto Rico has had a difficult history.

_____ b. The relationship between Puerto Rico and the United States has evolved continuously since the United States acquired the island.

_____ c. Most of Puerto Rico's population can read.

Correct Answers, Part A _____

Correct Answers, Part B _____

Total Correct Answers _____

After the Revolutionary War, the United States became a new nation. As a nation, it needed a capital. Planning the city was a major task. The city had to be grand. It had to be a symbol to the world.

In 1790 George Washington chose the site for the capital. It was on the banks of the Potomac River. It was in the center of the 13 states. It was also near the Atlantic coast. The city needed to be near the ocean so that it would be easy to trade with Europe.

The next step was to choose a designer for the city. Washington chose Pierre L'Enfant. L'Enfant was a French engineer. He loved the new country. He wrote to Washington and asked if he could be the city designer. In 1791 he finished the design. But he did not finish the project. He had a bad temper, so Washington fired him. L'Enfant took his plans with him when he left. Benjamin Banneker, an African American who was part of the design team, redrew the plans from memory. In 1792 crews laid the cornerstone for the White House.

L'Enfant's city plan was a diamond measuring 10 miles on each side. The city would have wide streets linking points of interest. The avenues in the city were set in diagonals. They branched out from the two main buildings in the city: the Capitol and the White House. L'Enfant used lots of open space in his plan. He wanted to connect with the natural landscape as much as he could. He thought a city should use its natural resources in its design.

In 1902 the city went through one more major change. Senator James McMillan put together a new design group. He wanted the group to design a large park system for the city. Group members looked back at the L'Enfant plan while doing their own work. They went to Europe for seven weeks. They were told to study the great capitals of Europe. McMillan wanted a European influence for the U.S. capital.

The committee members made big plans for the city. They created a complete park system. They chose sites for government buildings. They improved the Mall area and cleaned up the city. As time went on, the city added more museums and monuments. Together, two great plans helped create the city that visitors now see.

Reading Time _____

Recalling Facts

1. The site for the capital city was chosen by
   - ❏ a. Andrew Ellicott.
   - ❏ b. Pierre L'Enfant.
   - ❏ c. George Washington.

2. The nation's capital needed to be close to the ocean because of
   - ❏ a. a food shortage.
   - ❏ b. trade with Europe.
   - ❏ c. the healthy climate.

3. The original city plan was redrawn by
   - ❏ a. Pierre L'Enfant.
   - ❏ b. James McMillan.
   - ❏ c. Benjamin Banneker.

4. The L'Enfant plan
   - ❏ a. used lots of open spaces in the design.
   - ❏ b. was complex and hard to understand.
   - ❏ c. did not incorporate natural resources into the design.

5. James McMillan sent his design team to Europe because he
   - ❏ a. thought European cities were more interesting.
   - ❏ b. wanted Washington's design to have a European influence.
   - ❏ c. believed that the design team would work better if they had a vacation.

Understanding Ideas

6. One can conclude from the passage that L'Enfant
   - ❏ a. had many friends.
   - ❏ b. was easy to work with.
   - ❏ c. had good skills as an engineer but was difficult to work with.

7. One can conclude from the passage that the city planning process for Washington, D.C.,
   - ❏ a. was a smooth and easy one.
   - ❏ b. had many difficulties to overcome.
   - ❏ c. was completed in a short period of time.

8. A person designing a city plan in the eighteenth century would most likely use
   - ❏ a. a personal computer.
   - ❏ b. pen and ink on paper.
   - ❏ c. a camera for aerial photography.

9. One can conclude from the passage that a city's design plan is often
   - ❏ a. developed by many sources.
   - ❏ b. created by one person who has many skills.
   - ❏ c. exactly the same way for many centuries to come.

10. Which of the following sentences best tells what the whole passage is about?
    - ❏ a. Washington, D.C., is one of the grand capitals of the world.
    - ❏ b. Two plans helped create the Washington, D.C., of today.
    - ❏ c. Senator McMillan wanted a European influence on the capital city.

The Lincoln Memorial is located in Washington, D.C. It is a tribute to Abraham Lincoln. He was the sixteenth president of the United States. During the Civil War, Lincoln had helped keep the Union strong. But he was killed in 1865, just days after the war ended. The structure was built to honor Lincoln's work during the Civil War. In 1914 work began on the memorial. It was finished in 1922.

The building looks like a Greek temple. It has 36 columns. Each column stands for one of the 36 states that were part of the union when Lincoln was president. The building contains stones from many states. The outside is made of marble from Colorado. Limestone from Indiana is on the inside walls. Pink marble from Tennessee is on the floor. Marble from Alabama is on the ceiling.

Many inscriptions are on the walls. The Gettysburg Address is on the south wall. There is also a mural on that wall. It shows the angel of truth freeing an enslaved person. All these things have to do with ideas that Lincoln cherished. The statue of Lincoln is in the center of the building. It is 19 feet tall and 19 feet wide. It is made of 28 blocks of marble. The statue faces a long pool of water.

1. **Recognizing Words in Context**

Find the word *cherished* in the passage. One definition below is closest to the meaning of that word. One definition has the opposite or nearly the opposite meaning. The remaining definition has a completely different meaning. Label the definitions C for *closest*, O for *opposite or nearly opposite*, and D for *different*.

_____ a. disliked

_____ b. created

_____ c. valued

2. **Distinguishing Fact from Opinion**

Two of the statements below present *facts*, which can be proved. The other statement is an *opinion*, which expresses someone's thoughts or beliefs. Label the statements F for *fact* and O for *opinion*.

_____ a. Lincoln was the greatest U.S. President.

_____ b. Lincoln helped preserve the Union during the Civil War.

_____ c. Lincoln was killed soon after the Civil War ended.

3. Keeping Events in Order

Number the statements below 1, 2, and 3 to show the order in which the events took place.

_____ a. Lincoln was elected president.

_____ b. Work began on the Lincoln Memorial.

_____ c. Lincoln was killed.

4. Making Correct Inferences

Two of the statements below are correct *inferences,* or reasonable guesses. They are based on information in the passage. The other statement is an incorrect, or faulty, inference. Label the statements C for *correct* inference and F for *faulty* inference.

_____ a. Lincoln valued equality and justice.

_____ b. The Lincoln Memorial is designed like a Greek temple because Lincoln had studied in Greece.

_____ c. Lincoln is one of the most famous U.S. presidents.

5. Understanding Main Ideas

One of the statements below expresses the main idea of the passage. One statement is too general, or too broad. The other explains only part of the passage; it is too narrow. Label the statements M for *main idea*, B for *too broad*, and N for *too narrow*.

_____ a. The Lincoln Memorial is a beautiful tribute to the sixteenth U.S. President.

_____ b. The Lincoln Memorial contains a statue of Lincoln.

_____ c. The Lincoln Memorial is one of many monuments in Washington, D.C.

Correct Answers, Part A _____

Correct Answers, Part B _____

Total Correct Answers _____

100

Many people lived in the United States before the settlers came from Europe. These ancient peoples had complex cultures. One trait of these cultures was their strong tie to the land. The people used the land for many things. One thing people did with the land was create mounds. Scientists have found mounds built by many different groups of native people. They called the people who built these mounds "Mound Builders."

Three cultures seem to have built most of the mounds found in the United States. These cultures are the Adena, the Hopewell, and the Mississippian. Each culture contains many groups. Of the three, the Adena culture is the oldest. It was located mainly in Ohio. The mounds from this culture date back to 1000 B.C. The Hopewell culture rose as the Adena culture was dying. The Hopewell moved as far south as Florida. This culture seemed more informal. The groups worked with one another as trading partners. This culture lasted about 700 years. The most recent and most advanced culture is the Mississippian. This culture had a complex religious and social structure.

Mounds can be found in many parts of the country—from New York to Florida. They are found as far west as Nebraska. No one knows for sure just why the mounds were built.

There appear to be three main types of mounds. They are the temple mounds, the burial mounds, and the effigy mounds. The temple mounds are the oldest mounds. People may have built temples or places of worship on top of the mounds. People would climb ramps to reach the temple for worship. Some mounds had the homes of leaders built on top of them. Other mounds were burial mounds. The burial mounds were most likely built to honor the dead. Scientists have found skeletons and jewelry in some of these mounds. Effigy mounds are mounds shaped like animals, such as serpents or birds.

Each mound took many years to build. Many people worked together. People would work from dawn to dusk. They would gather baskets of dirt. Then they would go to the place where the mound was to be built and dump the dirt. They would stamp the dirt down with their feet. Then they would gather more dirt. This would go on day after day until a shape emerged. Mound building probably went on for about 5,500 years in North America.

Reading Time _____

Recalling Facts

1. The oldest culture of mound builders in the United States is the
   - ❑ a. Adena.
   - ❑ b. Hopewell.
   - ❑ c. Mississippian.

2. The most complex of the mound builder cultures is the
   - ❑ a. Adena.
   - ❑ b. Hopewell.
   - ❑ c. Mississippian.

3. The Hopewell culture was located primarily in
   - ❑ a. Ohio.
   - ❑ b. Florida.
   - ❑ c. Mississippi.

4. The three main types of mounds are burial mounds, temple mounds, and
   - ❑ a. effigy mounds.
   - ❑ b. serpent mounds.
   - ❑ c. worship mounds.

5. The mounds were made by
   - ❑ a. wind and water erosion.
   - ❑ b. very complex machines.
   - ❑ c. many people working together.

Understanding Ideas

6. One can conclude from the passage that the mounds were
   - ❑ a. not part of daily life for ancient people.
   - ❑ b. an important part of the life of ancient people.
   - ❑ c. designed to provide a window into history for modern man.

7. It is likely that the people building the mounds
   - ❑ a. were elderly people.
   - ❑ b. were not in very good shape.
   - ❑ c. were used to heavy physical labor.

8. The shapes of the effigy mounds were probably
   - ❑ a. important symbols to the mound builders.
   - ❑ b. randomly chosen by the mound builders.
   - ❑ c. unimportant to the mound builders.

9. One can conclude from the passage that the people who built the mounds
   - ❑ a. were unorganized.
   - ❑ b. were dedicated to their task.
   - ❑ c. built mounds in their spare time.

10. One can conclude from the passage that
    - ❑ a. each mound could be built in a day.
    - ❑ b. the mounds took a long time to build.
    - ❑ c. the mounds were built to look exactly the same.

23 | B | A Visit to Effigy Mounds National Monument

Effigy Mounds National Monument is located in Iowa. The park contains almost 200 mounds. The mounds have many shapes. Some of the mounds here are cone-shaped. These are the oldest ones. Other mounds look like long lines. There are also about 30 effigy mounds in the park. An effigy is a shape that looks like a living thing, such as a bird or a bear. The mounds have various sizes. One of the biggest is the Great Bear Mound. It is 137 feet long, 70 feet across, and 3.5 feet high.

Many native groups made mounds. Mounds can be found throughout the United States. The oldest mounds in Effigy Mounds National Park were built about 500 B.C. Tools and weapons have been found in the mounds. They teach scientists how the mound builders lived. They show how the people hunted and how they made their houses and clothes.

The park also has a unique natural landscape. Its environment is more diverse than the environment of any other U.S. national park. The area has forests, tallgrass prairies, wetlands, and rivers. The park is home to beavers, muskrats, and red-shouldered hawks. Oak and aspen trees are found in the park. The park became a national monument in 1949. In 1961 it became a land and wildlife preserve.

1. **Recognizing Words in Context**

   Find the word *diverse* in the passage. One definition below is closest to the meaning of that word. One definition has the opposite or nearly the opposite meaning. The remaining definition has a completely different meaning. Label the definitions C for *closest*, O for *opposite or nearly opposite*, and D for *different*.

   _____ a. beautiful

   _____ b. varied

   _____ c. similar

2. **Distinguishing Fact from Opinion**

   Two of the statements below present *facts*, which can be proved. The other statement is an *opinion*, which expresses someone's thoughts or beliefs. Label the statements F for *fact* and O for *opinion*.

   _____ a. The mounds were built by many native groups.

   _____ b. Effigy Mounds National Monument has a unique natural landscape.

   _____ c. The effigy mounds are the most interesting mounds in the United States.

3. Keeping Events in Order

Number the statements below 1, 2, and 3 to show the order in which the events took place.

_____ a. Effigy Mounds Park became a wildlife preserve.

_____ b. Effigy Mounds Park became a national monument.

_____ c. Mound building began in Iowa.

4. Making Correct Inferences

Two of the statements below are correct *inferences,* or reasonable guesses. They are based on information in the passage. The other statement is an incorrect, or faulty, inference. Label the statements C for *correct* inference and F for *faulty* inference.

_____ a. Effigy mounds have the most significance for ancient people.

_____ b. The bear was most likely an important symbol to ancient people.

_____ c. Many people today are fascinated by the ancient mounds.

5. Understanding Main Ideas

One of the statements below expresses the main idea of the passage. One statement is too general, or too broad. The other explains only part of the passage; it is too narrow. Label the statements M for *main idea,* B for *too broad,* and N for *too narrow.*

_____ a. One of the biggest mounds in Effigy Mounds National Monument is Great Bear Mound.

_____ b. Effigy Mounds National Monument offers visitors a glimpse at ancient mound-builder cultures within a beautiful landscape.

_____ c. National parks such as Effigy Mounds National Monument are exciting places to visit.

Correct Answers, Part A _____

Correct Answers, Part B _____

Total Correct Answers _____

In the United States, people can obtain official government posts in two ways. One way is by being appointed. The other is by being elected. The public casts votes to elect people to key posts. People elected to federal posts include the president and members of Congress. Those elected to state posts include the governor and state legislators. Those elected to local posts include the mayor and members of the school board. People who compete for office are called candidates. To obtain these posts, they must win an election.

Candidates work hard to gain the support of the people. They run campaigns aimed at winning votes. In their campaigns, they present their views. They want the public to know what they stand for. They want to show that the concerns of the public are their concerns. They hope to convey that they are the best choice for the post.

To reach the public, candidates use varied methods. For state and local posts, they send out pamphlets. Campaign workers phone voters or reach them door to door. Public forums give the voters a chance to meet and talk with those running for office. The press aids the candidates. News programs and newspapers report on the campaigns. Some TV and radio stations broadcast interviews. Local campaigns last for a few months.

A campaign for president is different. Those who run for this office campaign for more than a year. They need to reach voters across the nation. Travel is important. Rallies in large cities gather voter support. Meetings each day with the press spread the campaign message. Debates give candidates a chance to argue their views. Campaigns of this size call for the aid of thousands of workers.

Most of those who run for president belong to a political party. Just one member of each party can run for president. Each party names its candidate. Sometimes a preliminary election, or a primary, helps the party make its choice. Most states hold primary elections. Voters in each state cast their ballots to decide who they want to be their party's candidate. Later the party names the official candidate. This person goes on to run against the candidates of other parties. The one who earns the most public support is the one who receives the most votes. In the end, it is often the best campaign that wins the election.

Reading Time _____

Recalling Facts

1. Someone gains an office in
   - ❑ a. a debate.
   - ❑ b. a campaign.
   - ❑ c. an election.

2. Those who compete for office are called
   - ❑ a. officials.
   - ❑ b. candidates.
   - ❑ c. political parties.

3. To gain the support of the people, candidates
   - ❑ a. run campaigns.
   - ❑ b. give out prizes.
   - ❑ c. join political parties.

4. Those who run for president need to reach voters
   - ❑ a. in person.
   - ❑ b. across the nation.
   - ❑ c. in a few weeks' time.

5. Just one member of each party can run for
   - ❑ a. Congress.
   - ❑ b. president.
   - ❑ c. the school board.

Understanding Ideas

6. One can conclude from the passage that the purpose of a campaign is to
   - ❑ a. pass laws.
   - ❑ b. raise funds.
   - ❑ c. gather support from voters.

7. Compared with campaigns for local posts, a campaign for president requires
   - ❑ a. more time.
   - ❑ b. less money.
   - ❑ c. fewer workers.

8. It is likely that travel is vital for candidates for president because they need to
   - ❑ a. take lots of vacations.
   - ❑ b. gain nationwide support.
   - ❑ c. visit many foreign countries.

9. One can conclude from the passage that sending pamphlets, meeting with the press, and holding debates are
   - ❑ a. campaign methods.
   - ❑ b. duties of the president.
   - ❑ c. jobs of school board members.

10. One can conclude from the passage that the more public support one gains,
   - ❑ a. the less a campaign aids a candidate.
   - ❑ b. the greater the chance of winning an election.
   - ❑ c. the more likely that other candidates will drop out of the race.

The United States is a democracy. The government gains its power from the people. The people elect leaders to run the nation. A democracy gives the people many rights. One of the most basic rights is the right to vote. When a person votes, he or she asserts the voice of the people. Voting preserves the rights and power of the people. President Lyndon Johnson once said that without the right to vote, no other right would have any meaning.

People vote for many reasons. Some go to the polls to choose leaders. They vote to elect people to office. Their votes grant the leaders the power to rule. In this way, the people consent to be governed. Others vote to play a part in their government. They believe their ballots have an impact on the fate of the nation. In some elections, people cast votes to settle local issues. Often these matters affect daily life. They may vote on public transport or the building of a new school. They mark their ballots to express their views. Their votes shape the future of their towns and districts. On all levels, the right to vote grants the people the power of self-rule.

1. **Recognizing Words in Context**

Find the word *consent* in the passage. One definition below is closest to the meaning of that word. One definition has the opposite or nearly the opposite meaning. The remaining definition has a completely different meaning. Label the definitions C for *closest*, O for *opposite or nearly opposite*, and D for *different*.

_____ a. agree

_____ b. refuse

_____ c. suggest

2. **Distinguishing Fact from Opinion**

Two of the statements below present *facts*, which can be proved. The other statement is an *opinion*, which expresses someone's thoughts or beliefs. Label the statements F for *fact* and O for *opinion*.

_____ a. Without the right to vote, no rights would have any meaning.

_____ b. People vote to elect officials to public office.

_____ c. One of the basic rights in a democracy is the right to vote.

3. Keeping Events in Order

Two of the statements below describe events that happened at the same time. The other statement describes an event that happened before or after those events. Label two statements S for *same time*. Then label one statement B for *before* or A for *after*.

_____ a. People cast votes to settle a local issue.

_____ b. People cast votes to select the nation's leaders.

_____ c. In a democracy, people are born as citizens, or they ask to become citizens.

4. Making Correct Inferences

Two of the statements below are correct *inferences,* or reasonable guesses. They are based on information in the passage. The other statement is an incorrect, or faulty, inference. Label the statements C for *correct* inference and F for *faulty* inference.

_____ a. Regardless of why people vote, their votes have an impact.

_____ b. The people grant the government power in a democracy.

_____ c. Voting has no impact on the state of the nation.

5. Understanding Main Ideas

One of the statements below expresses the main idea of the passage. One statement is too general, or too broad. The other explains only part of the passage; it is too narrow. Label the statements M for *main idea*, B for *too broad*, and N for *too narrow*.

_____ a. A democracy is ruled by the people for the people.

_____ b. In some elections, people cast votes to settle local issues.

_____ c. By voting, people grant power to leaders and express their views.

Correct Answers, Part A _____

Correct Answers, Part B _____

Total Correct Answers _____

The Six Landform Regions of Canada

The nation of Canada lies to the north of the United States. It is a land of varied natural features. Distinct landforms divide the nation into six regions.

The Atlantic region spans the eastern coast of Canada. An old mountain range makes this region hilly and rugged. Valleys run between the hills. People farm in these valleys. The land there is sheltered from the wind of the Atlantic Ocean. Off the coast is one of the best fishing grounds in the world. It is called the Grand Banks. Here cold currents from the north meet warm currents from the south.

The Great Lakes and Lowlands are inland from the eastern coast. This region shares with the United States five lakes called the Great Lakes. This is the largest group of freshwater lakes in the world. Long ago flowing rivers of ice, called glaciers, covered the region. As they melted, huge lakes formed. Over time, some of these lakes drained. They left behind layers of rich sediment. This fertile soil is excellent for farming.

Farther west is the Canadian Shield. This is a dome of rock that covers almost half of the nation. There is little soil in this region. However, forests persist amid the rock. Grassy bogs, lakes, and rivers are also abundant.

In the interior of the country are the Plains. The forests of the north give way to prairies of tall grass. Farmers here grow grain crops such as wheat. Farther south, the dry climate allows for only low grasses. This area is perfect for raising cattle.

On the western coast of Canada is the Cordillera. This is a region of stark contrasts. Not far from the grassy plains are ice fields, glaciers, and high mountain peaks. This region lies between two mountain ranges. They are the Rocky Mountains and the Coastal Mountains. Other landforms include deep gorges, high plateaus, and steep coastal cliffs. Despite the harsh landscape, forests abound. People even farm in the valleys between the ranges.

The uppermost part of the nation is called the North or the Tundra. This region lies in the Arctic Circle. The winters are long and dark, and the summers are short and cool. This region borders the icy waters of the Arctic Ocean. Except for the top layer of soil, the ground is frozen year round. There are no trees and little plant life. This region is unlike any other in Canada.

Reading Time _____

Recalling Facts

1. The nation of Canada lies to the north of the
   - ❑ a. Arctic Circle.
   - ❑ b. United States.
   - ❑ c. Coastal Mountains.

2. Distinct landforms divide the nation into
   - ❑ a. two regions.
   - ❑ b. six regions.
   - ❑ c. hundreds of regions.

3. The Grand Banks fishing ground is off the coast of the
   - ❑ a. Atlantic region.
   - ❑ b. interior plains.
   - ❑ c. Cordillera mountain ranges.

4. The dome of rock that covers almost half of the nation is the
   - ❑ a. Canadian Shield.
   - ❑ b. Rocky Mountain range.
   - ❑ c. Grand Banks fishing ground.

5. The ground is frozen year round in the
   - ❑ a. Great Lakes.
   - ❑ b. Canadian Shield.
   - ❑ c. North, or the Tundra.

Understanding Ideas

6. One can conclude from the passage that the region known for its fields, grasses, and grain crops is the
   - ❑ a. Plains.
   - ❑ b. Tundra.
   - ❑ c. Cordillera.

7. One can conclude from the passage that the freshwater Great Lakes was made
   - ❑ a. by melting glaciers.
   - ❑ b. from an ancient ocean.
   - ❑ c. from the largest river in the world.

8. One can infer that the Atlantic region on Canada's eastern coast is named for the
   - ❑ a. Arctic Circle.
   - ❑ b. Atlantic Ocean.
   - ❑ c. city of Atlantis.

9. It is likely that Lake Superior, on the border of Canada and the United States, is in the
   - ❑ a. Tundra.
   - ❑ b. Canadian Shield.
   - ❑ c. Great Lakes and Lowland region.

10. One can conclude that the gorges, plateaus, sea cliffs, and valleys of the Cordillera are a product of the region's
    - ❑ a. forests.
    - ❑ b. glaciers.
    - ❑ c. mountain ranges.

25 B The Art and Sport of Ice and Snow Sculpture

Ice carving and snow sculpting are sports as well as arts. The Great Lakes region of the United States and Canada hosts contests in these sports each winter. The region is a perfect site for these events. It has long cold winters and ample snowfall. The sculptures are works of art.

Ice carving is an art. Ice sculptures range from massive monuments to small decorations. The artists who make them may be sculptors or chefs. But ice carving is also a sport. Contests may last for days. Teams of two or more people sculpt blocks of ice the size of large suitcases. At some contests a team works on one block of ice. At other contests, a team may create a sculpture from 25 blocks of ice.

The art of snow sculpting attracts sculptors who normally work with other materials. They enjoy working with snow because they can make massive forms in a short time. In contests, teams of three or four people sculpt one large snow block. The blocks may be the size of a small room. They may weigh 35 tons. These contests last for two to five days. Artists work day and night to finish on time. Once completed, the snow sculptures are displayed. The sculptures remain on view as long as the cold weather lasts.

1. **Recognizing Words in Context**

   Find the word *ample* in the passage. One definition below is closest to the meaning of that word. One definition has the opposite or nearly the opposite meaning. The remaining definition has a completely different meaning. Label the definitions C for *closest*, O for *opposite or nearly opposite*, and D for *different*.

   _____ a. bright

   _____ b. plenty

   _____ c. not enough

2. **Distinguishing Fact from Opinion**

   Two of the statements below present *facts*, which can be proved. The other statement is an *opinion*, which expresses someone's thoughts or beliefs. Label the statements F for *fact* and O for *opinion*.

   _____ a. Ice carvers are often sculptors or chefs.

   _____ b. An ice carving is more elegant than a snow sculpture.

   _____ c. At some ice carving contests, teams make massive sculptures from 25 blocks of ice.

3. Keeping Events in Order

Number the statements below 1, 2, and 3 to show the order in which the events took place.

_____ a. The snow sculptures remain on view as long as the cold weather lasts.

_____ b. Well-packed blocks of snow the size of a small room are ready for each team.

_____ c. Teams of three or four people work day and night to complete their sculptures in time.

4. Making Correct Inferences

Two of the statements below are correct *inferences,* or reasonable guesses. They are based on information in the passage. The other statement is an incorrect, or faulty, inference. Label the statements C for *correct* inference and F for *faulty* inference.

_____ a. Snow sculpting is mainly an outdoor event.

_____ b. Fewer artists sculpt with ice than snow.

_____ c. Ice carving and snow sculpting contests often are held in the northern part of the United States.

5. Understanding Main Ideas

One of the statements below expresses the main idea of the passage. One statement is too general, or too broad. The other explains only part of the passage; it is too narrow. Label the statements M for *main idea,* B for *too broad,* and N for *too narrow.*

_____ a. Sculpture is a varied art form.

_____ b. Ice carving and snow sculpting are sports as well as arts.

_____ c. The Great Lakes region of the United States and Canada is perfect for snow and ice sculpture.

Correct Answers, Part A _____

Correct Answers, Part B _____

Total Correct Answers _____

ANSWER KEY

READING RATE GRAPH

COMPREHENSION SCORE GRAPH

COMPREHENSION SKILLS PROFILE GRAPH

ANSWER KEY

1A	1. c	2. b	3. b	4. c	5. b	6. c	7. c	8. a	9. c	10. b
1B	1. D, C, O	2. F, F, O	3. 2, 1, 3	4. F, C, C	5. B, N, M					
2A	1. c	2. b	3. b	4. c	5. a	6. a	7. b	8. c	9. b	10. c
2B	1. D, O, C	2. F, O, F	3. 1, 2, 3	4. C, F, C	5. B, N, M,					
3A	1. b	2. b	3. b	4. c	5. b	6. c	7. a	8. a	9. b	10. b
3B	1. D, C, O	2. F, O, F	3. 2, 1, 3	4. C, F, C	5. M, N, B					
4A	1. a	2. c	3. a	4. a	5. c	6. c	7. b	8. a	9. b	10. c
4B	1. O, C, D	2. F, O, F	3. 3, 2, 1	4. F, C, C	5. N, B, M					
5A	1. a	2. c	3. a	4. c	5. b	6. b	7. c	8. a	9. b	10. c
5B	1. D, C, O	2. O, F, F	3. 3, 2, 1	4. C, F, C	5. M, N, B					
6A	1. b	2. a	3. a	4. b	5. c	6. b	7. a	8. b	9. c	10. b
6B	1. C, O, D	2. O, F, F	3. 3, 1, 2	4. C, F, C	5. B, N, M					
7A	1. b	2. b	3. a	4. c	5. b	6. b	7. b	8. c	9. a	10. c
7B	1. D, C, O	2. O, F, F	3. 3, 2, 1	4. C, F, C	5. N, B, M					
8A	1. c	2. a	3. b	4. a	5. b	6. b	7. a	8. a	9. c	10. a
8B	1. C, O, D	2. F, F, O	3. 2, 3, 1	4. F, C, C	5. N, B, M					
9A	1. c	2. b	3. a	4. a	5. b	6. a	7. b	8. b	9. c	10. c
9B	1. D, O, C	2. F, F, O	3. 1, 3, 2	4. C, C, F	5. N, B, M					
10A	1. a	2. b	3. b	4. a	5. b	6. c	7. b	8. b	9. a	10. c
10B	1. O, D, C	2. F, F, 0	3. 3, 1, 2	4. C, F, C	5. M, N, B					
11A	1. a	2. a	3. b	4. b	5. a	6. b	7. c	8. b	9. c	10. a
11B	1. O, C, D	2. F, O, F	3. 1, 2, 3	4. F, C, C	5. M, B, N					
12A	1. b	2. c	3. b	4. a	5. c	6. b	7. a	8. c	9. b	10. a
12B	1. O, C, D	2. F, F, O	3. 3, 1, 2	4. C, F, C	5. N, B, M					
13A	1. a	2. b	3. a	4. a	5. b	6. a	7. a	8. a	9. c	10. b
13B	1. O, D, C	2. O, F, F	3. 2, 1, 3	4. F, C, C	5. N, M, B					

14A	1. c	2. c	3. b	4. b	5. c	6. c	7. a	8. a	9. b	10. b
14B	1. O, C, D	2. F, O, F	3. 3, 2, 1	4. C, F, C	5. M, B, N					
15A	1. a	2. a	3. c	4. b	5. a	6. b	7. a	8. c	9. c	10. a
15B	1. D, C, O	2. F, F, O	3. 2, 1, 3	4. F, C, C	5. M, N, B					
16A	1. b	2. a	3. c	4. a	5. c	6. c	7. b	8. c	9. a	10. c
16B	1. O, D, C	2. O, F, F	3. 3, 1, 2	4. C, C, F	5. B, N, M					
17A	1. c	2. a	3. b	4. b	5. a	6. b	7. c	8. c	9. a	10. b
17B	1. C, D, O	2. F, O, F	3. 1, 2, 3	4. C, F, C	5. M, B, N					
18A	1. c	2. a	3. c	4. c	5. b	6. a	7. c	8. c	9. c	10. b
18B	1. D, C, O	2. F, F, O	3. 2, 1, 3	4. C, C, F	5. M, N, B					
19A	1. a	2. a	3. a	4. b	5. a	6. c	7. a	8. a	9. b	10. a
19B	1. D, O, C	2. O, F, F	3. 2, 3, 1	4. F, C, C	5. N, M, B					
20A	1. a	2. c	3. b	4. b	5. c	6. b	7. c	8. c	9. a	10. c
20B	1. O, C, D	2. F, O, F	3. 3, 2, 1	4. C, F, C	5. M, N, B					
21A	1. b	2. a	3. b	4. c	5. c	6. c	7. b	8. b	9. b	10. c
21B	1. D, O, C	2. F, F, O	3. 3, 1, 2	4. C, C, F	5. B, M, N					
22A	1. c	2. b	3. c	4. a	5. b	6. c	7. b	8. b	9. a	10. b
22B	1. O, D, C	2. O, F, F	3. 1, 3, 2	4. C, F, C	5. M, N, B					
23A	1. a	2. c	3. b	4. a	5. c	6. b	7. c	8. a	9. b	10. b
23B	1. D, C, O	2. F, F, O	3. 3, 2, 1	4. F, C, C	5. N, M, B					
24A	1. c	2. b	3. a	4. b	5. b	6. c	7. a	8. b	9. a	10. b
24B	1. C, O, D	2. O, F, F	3. S, S, B	4. C, C, F	5. B, N, M					
25A	1. b	2. b	3. a	4. a	5. c	6. a	7. a	8. b	9. c	10. c
25B	1. D, C, O	2. F, O, F	3. 3, 1, 2	4. C, F, C	5. B, M, N					

Reading Rate

Put an X on the line above each lesson number to show your reading time and words-per-minute rate for that lesson.

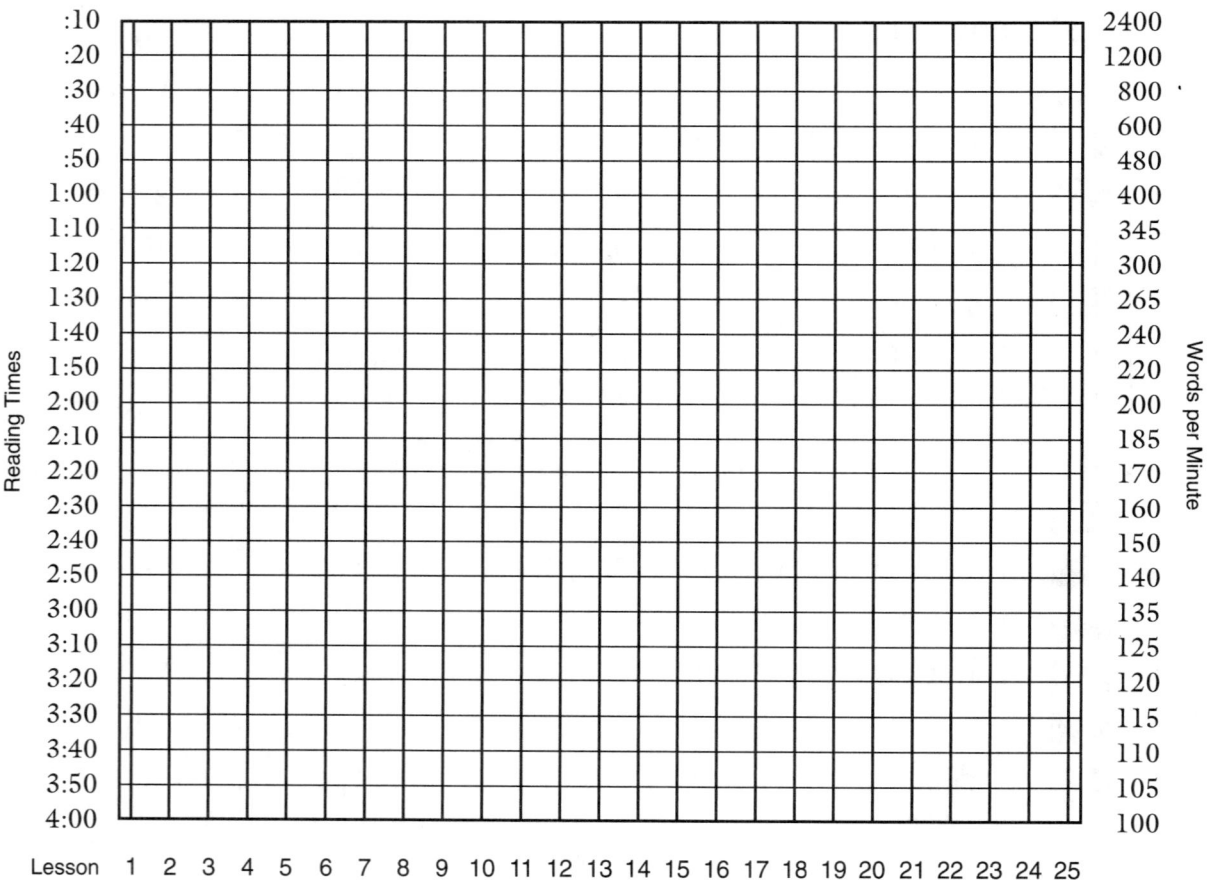

Reading Times		Words per Minute
:10		2400
:20		1200
:30		800
:40		600
:50		480
1:00		400
1:10		345
1:20		300
1:30		265
1:40		240
1:50		220
2:00		200
2:10		185
2:20		170
2:30		160
2:40		150
2:50		140
3:00		135
3:10		125
3:20		120
3:30		115
3:40		110
3:50		105
4:00		100

Lesson 1 2 3 4 5 6 7 8 9 10 11 12 13 14 15 16 17 18 19 20 21 22 23 24 25

COMPREHENSION SCORE

Put an X on the line above each lesson number to indicate your total correct answers
and comprehension score for that lesson.

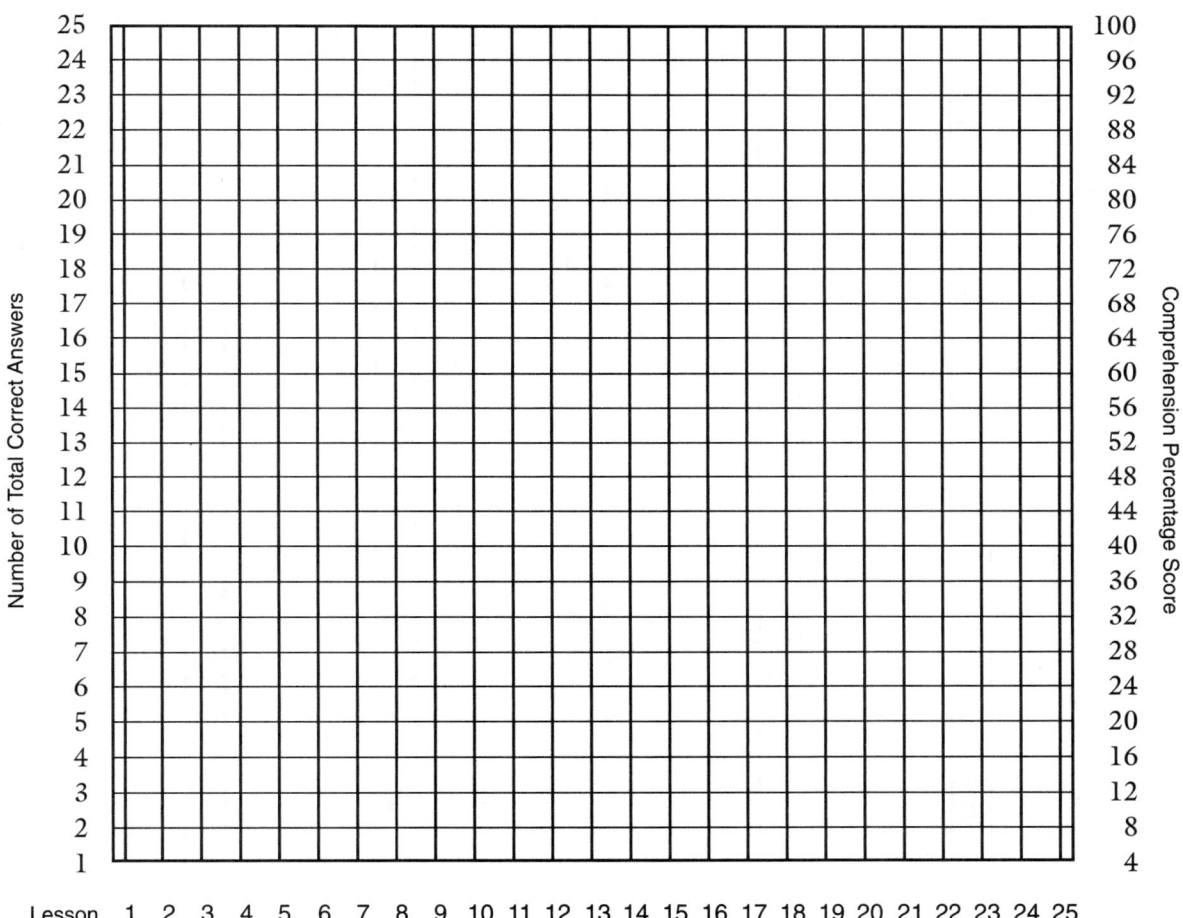

117

COMPREHENSION SKILLS PROFILE

Put an X in the box above each question type to indicate an incorrect reponse to any part of that question.

Lesson 1					
2					
3					
4					
5					
6					
7					
8					
9					
10					
11					
12					
13					
14					
15					
16					
17					
18					
19					
20					
21					
22					
23					
24					
25					
	Recognizing Words in Context	Distinguishing Fact from Opinion	Keeping Events in Order	Making Correct Inferences	Understanding Main Ideas